CHRISTIAN FAITH
AND PASTORAL CARE

CHRISTIAN FAITH

AND PASTORAL CARE

Charles Duell Kean

GREENWICH · CONNECTICUT · 1961

To ARTHUR CARL LICHTENBERGER,

Friend for many years, Pastor and Bishop

FOREWORD

Thoughtful men have always sensed, however dimly, that in the deeper levels of the human mind there are vast untapped resources for achieving the inner security that transcends all human feelings. Through the ages, men have sought access to the mysterious labyrinths of human nature, hoping to find the means by which people can experience more of the goodness of life instead of so much of its misery and anguish. Paradoxically, as the search has been pursued, intensified, and extended on many different levels of inquiry, the efforts have yielded not the finite proof of the nature of man but rather more evidence of how infinite is nature and infinitesimal our knowledge of man in it. But to twentieth-century science can be credited, I believe, the germ of fresh and leavening insight into the organic-social matrix from which evolves the character and personality of the individual—the conception of man's essential plasticity and uniqueness, his biological endowment guided, inhibited, shaped, and enhanced through and by the endless and ongoing experiences with the people and the world about him.

With recognition of the myriad forces that influence the unfolding of human potential, scientists have been able to advance a number of credible theories describing how an individual is equipped to meet the world and partake, to a greater or lesser extent, of its satisfactions. As presently conceptualized, that exquisite and delicate mechanism we know as the human brain responds to a welter of features in our social and cultural environment—patterns of family relationship and child rearing, educational procedures, community structures, and economic, political, and religious ideologies. Added to these fundamental governing influences of behavior are the pervasive and threatening stresses that arise from fears of nuclear holocaust and from rapid social changes with attendant undercurrents of loneliness, insecurity, and estrangement among the family of man.

To succeed so eminently in writing a book which places Christian faith relationships in perspective and in harmony with contemporary psychological and social insights is to merit the accolade of clergy and laity alike. Only a sensitive and cogent man, one such as the Reverend Doctor Charles Duell Kean, could have produced this impressive volume. It required full understanding of and devotion to the biblical precepts which must guide the pastor in the fellowship he serves. It demanded scholarship and recourse to departments of knowledge as diverse as epistemology, theology, sociology, economics, law, medicine and psychology. It called for a dedicated servant of God who sees many unmet needs for pastoral care, and is concerned about the ways of making them available in modern society.

To Doctor Kean, it is urgent that the professional ministry turn its attention to examining the ways and means by which pastoral care can become a living, healing force in a world where so often there is a cleavage between what should be and what actually is. The basic task of clergymen today, writes Doctor Kean, is one of recovering a dynamic sense of the "why" of congregational life, expressed in ways which appreciate the realities of our times rather than trying to recapture the flavor of an earlier age. To this end, he recommends responsible use of the serious studies in psychology and the social sciences, so that clergymen can assist men out of their webs of confusion and torment into activities whereby they can channel their energies constructively.

As a psychiatrist, I have found an extra profit in Doctor Kean's sound and considered work. One sometimes hears it mistakenly stated that psychiatry and allied sciences are antithetical to religion, that the sciences are at cross purposes to religious concepts of self-actualization. In point of fact, mental health values and Judaic-Christian doctrine travel along parallel, even converging paths. With sharp awareness of the pastor's responsibility in ministering to the sick and the troubled, Doctor Kean looks to the specialized knowledge and techniques of psychiatry, social agencies, and professional counselors in human relations not as a substitute for the pastor's never-ending task of mediating love and care, but as necessary adjuncts to it. As Doctor Kean points out, no political, economic, sociological, or technological development could make the Christian faith irrelevant or interfere with its mission, but such developments could help the Church speak and function more effectively in these anxious times. The meeting of psychological, social, and therapeutic sciences under the auspices of the Church serves to remind Christians that God's message can be communicated through secular as well as religious channels.

One of the most significant and promising developments in psychiatry in the last few years has been the emergence of the concepts of social psychiatry. In a very ample sense, the field of social psychiatry comprises all those areas where mental illness and the functioning of society are contiguous, including community administration and institutions of organized religion, law, school, and the family.

In a more specific sense, it refers to the variety of curative services which communities are now setting up for the treatment of the mentally ill, and for those in danger of becoming so. Many of the new community facilities are designed to serve either as an alternative to treatment in a mental hospital or as a means of shortening the period of hospitalization when it appears necessary. These services have also demonstrated their effectiveness in community programs of prevention and rehabilitation.

At the core of social psychiatry's concepts is the establishment of opportunities for the mental patient to make and renew with society contacts which are favorable to the maintenance or re-establishment of social adequacy. Interestingly, this new activity is new only in the sense that it represents a revival of interest in one of psychiatry's fundamental tenets; namely, that the distinguishing characteristic of the mentally healthy human being is his ability to create opportunities to collaborate and cooperate in human relationships and thus fulfill himself creatively. From life's inception to its end, man's destiny is inextricably linked with the destiny of other men. In the healing of minds and bodies, and in preventing their breakdown, the patient depends upon his physician for specialized knowledge, treatment, and diagnosis; but success in the conquest of any medical problem is dependent on the vast therapeutic aids which come only from people in the community at large, the great human assets which express themselves in a concern for the comfort and welfare of others.

Social psychiatry makes use of another long-recognized truth that man throughout his life is capable of changing. If his environment is supportive and favorable for him to act and behave constructively and cooperatively, he generally changes for the better and he enjoys mental health. When the environment fails to meet basic needs, the direction of change reverses, and the individual withdraws from the stream of life toward greater and greater deterioration in mental health. Psychiatry can bring many patients back to the threshold of normal living, and it can also successfully intervene in the development of psychiatric disorders. But all and any treatment efforts are for nothing if the community displays a hostile, mistrustful attitude toward the mentally ill and sustains the misconceptions and stigma that have long surrounded the diseases they suffer.

If the community attitudes are to be changed and the healing potential of a supportive community environment is to be utilized, the responsibility evolves upon every citizen. But society's caretakers—clergymen, teachers, physicians, those who make the laws and those who enforce them, and all the other people whose job it is to keep the wheels of a community going—must be in the vanguard of the efforts. With appropriate and sound orientation in mental health principles, these key people comprise a powerful therapeutic enterprise that can be a force for mental health as well as for the eradication of mental illness. They can give the substance to the hope that to mankind will come a better era of health and healing.

An adroit master of words as well as thought, Doctor Kean has brought together an impressive amount of information by which the various ministries of the Church can strengthen and enrich their services to individuals and families, and thereby help them toward interpersonal fulfillment.

ROBERT H. FELIX, M.D.

National Institute of Mental Health
Bethesda, Maryland

PREFACE

The ministry of pastoral care has acquired new dimensions in our day. Perhaps it would be more accurate to say that it has acquired a deeper appreciation of the dimensions which were already there.

The Christian Church has always been concerned with a ministry to individual persons; yet it has been aware that one never meets a person isolated either from the social factors which influence his life—family, job, community, world affairs—or from the history of experiences through which he has passed on his way to where he happens to be. Studies in sociology, economics and, above all, in depth psychology are making clear the realities which for centuries have been dimly felt to be significant. The Church seeks to make responsible use of the insights which are being acquired in our time and which are often developed under secular auspices. Yet in making use of these understandings the Church needs, at the same time, to focus much more clearly the faith-perspective in which they are employed.

This book is intended to be a meeting of the insights of Christian faith, as these have been developed through the ages, with the social and psychological understandings which are of such tremendous importance for the pastorate in our day. It is not intended to be a scientific or a "how to" book, though it will unavoidably have some suggestions in this area. Many able writers and thinkers have published their clinical experience in order to guide the pastoral ministry toward greater effectiveness, and their books are available to those who would study the theory and practice of pastoral ministrations.

The author does not pose as an expert. His entire ministry has been that of parish pastor rather than specialist. He has worked for more than twenty years with the ideas developed in this book, and when the Rev. Charles R. Stinnette, Associate Professor of Psychiatry and Religion at the Union Theological Seminary invited him to lecture there, it provided the stimulus which led eventually to the writing of this book.

During my ministry I have had many cooperative relationships with other clergy, physicians, psychiatrists, psychiatric caseworkers, and public health leaders. This experience has taught me that wherever the context of a common Christian faith can be understood and appreciated, cooperation is that much more effective. Even where such understanding and appreciation on a shared basis are impossible, because those with whom one works either belong to other religious traditions or have none at all, the minister's understanding of his own role is crucial in making this cooperation possible.

Our prime objective as clergymen is what has been traditionally known as "the cure of souls": concern and care for people because they are the children of God. This is an adventurous enterprise calling forth the greatest possible skills and personal dedication from both professional workers and laity. In the following chapters the cure of souls will be looked at primarily from the point of view of the clergyman, who is seeking both to do the most effective job for the welfare of those in his care, and to work in the closest fellowship with professionals from other disciplines as well as with lay partners.

To insure a clear understanding it will be necessary to define a few terms. Throughout the book, the basic term to describe the clergyman will be either *clergyman* or *minister*. The more specialized terms *priest, pastor,* and *preacher* will be used to refer to particular functions of the ministry. In the Episcopal Church, for instance, the word *priest* is often used as a synonym for *clergyman,* and in the Lutheran and other traditions the word *pastor* is so used, and in still other communions the word *preacher*. Therefore, I beg the indulgence of those who are accustomed to use these titles within a denominational frame of reference. We are interested here in describing the rationale of what clergymen do, and to restrict the terms *pastor, priest* and *preacher* for specific aspects of the fulfillment of their ministry.

There is another set of terms which requires some comment. From my point of view, clergymen have no function whatever except within the life of the Church; but the word *Church* itself requires dynamic terms to describe it, if our understanding is not to be too narrowly institutional. Within the following chapters two such phrases will be used, and I hope appreciated, as meaning what they mean to me. One is *the Holy People of God,* explained in detail in Chapter I, describing the Church's role as successor to Old Testament Israel and also its mission as proclaimer of God's saving purpose. The other term is *the Fellowship of the Holy Spirit,* explained in detail in Chapter II, describing the fact that, for Christians, God is understood to work through the Church's life as a whole rather than merely through the ordained ministry. Certainly these are not peculiar terms, but perhaps their use as now explained may help clergy and laity appreciate more deeply the context in which the pastoral responsibility is assumed and carried out.

Although I am an Episcopalian, and have never been anything else, I have always had the privilege of working closely with clergymen of other communions. I have found that in basic essentials their problems and needs are very much the same as my own. The difference between us, however, is not simply a matter of terminology. I am sure that this book will be of greater value to non-Episcopalians if I state frankly from the outset that the sacramental life as described and made possible by The Book of Common Prayer—the common resource of Episcopal clergy and laity—provides the context in which I live and work. I do not say that the tradition which I have inherited and share with fellow Episcopalians is the only truth there is; I know too well the contrary. But I do say that for me it makes sense. I therefore ask the non-Episcopalian reader to bear in mind that if he were writing such a book, he would write out of his own ethos, if it were to be an honest, useful book. Likewise, I must write against my background and tradition.

One of the difficulties with much valuable work done in recent years is that, in trying to relate Christian theology and the insights of modern psychotherapy, so much has been done apart from the faith-perspective of the Church. We are not dealing with abstract ideas: we are dealing with a corporate life. This life expresses itself in many ways, but finds one of its most important articulations in its liturgy—once the liturgy is understood as having its meaning only within a faith community. I do not understand how pastoral care can be fully exercised unless there is a liturgical context. Paul Tillich says that counseling must always take place against the background of the eternal; and without a dynamic participation in the liturgy this cannot be done.

Two major influences are responsible for the writing of this book. The first, and probably the most important, is the large number of individuals whom I have been privileged to know on the level of pastoral counseling. Our encounter has taught me more about my own role than almost any other experience. The other influence is the long association I have had with a number of clergymen who have been seriously concerned about the interaction of the Christian faith and analytical psychology as developed by Sigmund Freud and many of the second- and third-generation researchers in dynamic therapy. I began work with representatives of this group twenty-five years ago through a most rewarding association with the late Rev. Otis R. Rice, D.D., then Associate Rector of St. Thomas' Church, New York, and Instructor at The General Theological Seminary.

The number of people who have contributed to my thinking is not only far too long to print, but many would doubtless be overlooked if I were to attempt to make a list. I will only express my particular debt to the Presiding Bishop, the Rt. Rev. Arthur C. Lichtenberger, who has encouraged me in this project from the beginning; the Rev. Charles R. Stinnette; the Rev. William M. Baxter, Rector of St. Mark's Church, Washington; the Rev. Ernest E. Bruder, Protestant Chaplain of St. Elizabeth's Hospital, Washington; the Rev. S. Knox Kreutzer, Jr., Director of the Pastoral Institute, Washington; Dr. Robert M. Felix, Director of the National Institute of Mental Health, whose foreword is more than generous; Dr. Margaret Rioch, psychiatrist; Miss Marcelle Clark and Miss Evalyn G. Weller of the United States Department of Health, Education, and Welfare.

C. D. K.

CONTENTS

Contents

CHRISTIAN FAITH
AND PASTORAL CARE

THE PASTOR
IN THE CHURCH

Pastoral care begins with the biblical understanding that the concern of Almighty God for his people is the same as that of a shepherd for his flock. The twenty-third Psalm, *The Lord is my shepherd,* reflects this feeling. Jesus, in the parable of the Lost Sheep, sees God's concern for the problems of individuals in a way parallel to that of a shepherd for one of his flock which has strayed away. At the end of the First Century, the author of St. John's gospel gives us the picture of Christ the Good Shepherd, and this image has become one of the distinctive symbols of the Christian faith. The author of the first epistle of Peter says to his fellow members of the late first-century Church: *For ye were as sheep going astray; but are now returned unto the Shepherd and Bishop of your souls.*

The title "pastor" is derived from the Latin word for shepherd. Its almost universal use in western Christendom to describe the role of the clergy in the Church suggests that the ministry of pastoral care for people is the logical development of the biblical proclamation of God's concern for souls.

The ministry of pastoral care is the practical application

3

of this biblical faith as it has come to be worked out in congregational life. The Church as a whole has the responsibility of making God's care for persons known and appreciated in the world of practical affairs. The clergy, however, are not surrogates for God in this responsibility: they serve to focus in practical form the general responsibility of the fellowship in which they serve.

God's concern remains only a beautiful idea until those who take it seriously do something about it. Because, under God's guidance, the holy fellowship has developed a full-time ministry to take responsibility for seeing that its task in the world is carried out, it becomes one of the duties of that ministry to mediate God's loving concern to people.

The tragic price that the Church has paid for developing a full-time ministry is that both the clergy and the laity tend to think of pastoral responsibility as being an exclusively ministerial function. One current evidence of this is that when laymen become seriously committed to the Christian faith, they often think that they should resign from whatever occupation they are pursuing and get ordained—as if the full ministry of Christian love and service belonged only to clergymen. One of the great needs of the Church in this mid-period of the Twentieth Century is to develop understandings of how lawyers, doctors, teachers, social workers, salesmen, engineers, and the like, can have a meaningful ministry in their professions and, in so doing, carry out a major aspect of the pastoral responsibility of the Church.

Pastoral care, then, is a normal part of the Church's life, and the clergy understand that they must give a reasonable proportion of their time to it. If they appreciate adequately the connection of pastoral responsibility to the Christian faith, they will also be seeking for laymen to share this pastorate—not as helpers to lighten their load, but as partners in a grand enterprise across the whole social front.

Clergymen know that their parishioners and others will call upon them for pastoral services. Laymen generally expect to be able to avail themselves of this service, when they want it, to the extent that they have any glimmer of what pastoral services are. The basic understanding is this: (1) the Holy People of God, the fellowship of Christian people, as described in I Peter 2:9—*But ye are a chosen generation, a royal priesthood, an holy nation, a peculiar people*—is the normal channel through which the influence of the faith is brought to bear upon people in the daily affairs which concern them; (2) this Holy People, the Church, makes its influence felt practically in congregational life where minister and parishioners are associated in the task of proclaiming the Gospel to the world; (3) congregational life involves the concern of the fellowship which represents God for the individual members who are the children of God; and, (4) the detailed responsibility for this concern devolves in large measure upon the professional ministry.

The Christian faith and pastoral care go hand in hand. The Christian faith is that view of God's saving love for people, both as individuals and in social life, which revolutionizes man's way of living with himself, with other people, and with God. Pastoral care is the term describing how this faith is reflected in practical, day-by-day situations where Christians minister to each other's needs because of their living loyalty to Christ.

The word "pastor" is not only a title given to ordained clergymen, but also a term which points to the kind of relationship which Christians feel toward each other once they appreciate the dynamic of their faith. While the official ministers give full-time service to the pastorate and also, for practical purposes, focus the general meaning of pastorate, the note of loving and healing responsibility for one another within the framework of the faith applies to all Christian people.

In a derivative sense, "pastor" describes the kind of relationship that the clergy are meant to have with their people in the Church of God. It is derived from the pastoral responsibility of the Church as a whole, generally shared by all serious Christians, yet entrusted in large part for the carrying out of its details to the professional minister. The word suggests that Christian relationships are to be understood primarily as growing out of a concern for persons as persons, and that even worship—central as that may be to the Christian life—finds its particularly Christian emphasis in the personal contact between the Most High God and his children. His children, therefore, know each other and live with each other in the presence of the Most High. The term carries with it the note of loving concern for each other by people who have a God-given relationship to each other.

The Congregation

The Judaeo-Christian tradition is unique in the religions of the world for teaching its adherents that they belong to the Holy People of God—a race, a nation, a fellowship—which has been called into existence for the purpose of making God's love known to mankind as a whole. It is a very natural development from this underlying premise that the normal agency through which The Holy People of God function demonstrably in history is the congregation —parish or synagogue. The congregation is meant to be the visible, objective manifestation of the fellowship of God's people in local circumstances where people meet

6

and work and play. Pastoral care for individual persons is one of the necessary ways in which this congregational life makes its influence felt in society.

Because of this particular sense of direction on the part of the Holy People of God, the Judaeo-Christian tradition manifests its life in an institution—the congregation—which is unique in the religious development of mankind. By its very existence the congregation takes what might be only an ethical ideal of the way people ought to be related to each other and makes it a matter of practical day-by-day relationships.

People who belong to a congregation have a kind of relationship with the other members, a relationship which, at best, can be compared with the way the members of a family are connected to each other. They know each other, or at least they are meant to. (One may wonder how congregations with a membership running into the thousands can fulfill the function of family.) People within the congregation know that the basis of their relationship to each other is their common Christian faith—it can only incidentally and secondarily be on other grounds, such as neighborhood, economic or social class, or even profession. People within the congregation may count on the sympathy and support of the other members when they need it, and the congregation on its own part has a sense of responsible concern for the welfare of those who comprise it.

Israel came to understand itself as the Holy People of God and to develop the synagogue as the normal expression of its religious life at one and the same time. While the roots of this understanding and this practice may be traced back for centuries, these came into their own in the period immediately following the Persian overthrow of the Babylonian Empire and the permission given to the Jewish people to return to Palestine if they wanted to. In the great poetic vision of what this opportunity might mean, the Deutero-Isaiah uses the picture of God as the shepherd: *He shall feed his flock like a shepherd: he shall gather the lambs with his arm, and carry them in his bosom, and shall gently lead those that are with young.*

Many religions at first glance seem to present this double note of God's agent in history and an internal fellowship between believers, but in the Judaeo-Christian tradition this understanding has a particular direction to it. The Holy People of God exist to serve the world through serving those who belong and through reaching out in loving care to those who have yet to find a place. This means that the local congregation itself exists to demonstrate this double function. The fellowship, of which the congregation is the local manifestation, finds its *raison d'être* not so much in its own privilege as in its responsibility for the welfare of people. Here the primary qualification for the Church's interest is not that particular men and women have a special status, but that living, human souls, born to be the children of God, need help.

It is in this sense that classical Judaism thought of itself as the moral and spiritual example for the nations, as this is reflected in the *Nunc dimittis,* the hymn of the ancient Simeon: *To be a light to lighten the Gentiles, and to be the glory of thy people Israel.* Indeed, Jesus' parable of the Good Samaritan was not really meant to tell people that they ought to be concerned with those who needed their care—there was no disagreement about the principle —but to point up to those who thought themselves outstanding in their religious loyalty that they were not really living up to what they claimed. Classical Christianity has always understood its mission to be the redemption of the whole world as the living Christ makes his influence felt through the expanding outreach of the Church. In this sense, pastoral care and missions are two sides of the same coin.

While the nature of the Church as the Holy People of God is interpreted in various ways in the different mainstream traditions of western Christendom, the basic teaching is universal. It is manifested again and again through public worship, and it is the presupposition underlying all institutional programs—educational, recreational and social welfare. Behind these various activities is the assumption: Those who are "in," that is, those who consciously and officially identify themselves with the Church, have a relationship with each other similar to that between the members of a family. In the Christian tradition there is a most important added element: those who do not feel themselves consciously "in" are wanted, and indeed it is felt that their lives will be seriously incomplete until they are helped to find their place within the heritage of God's love.

The congregation is the normal setting for the ministry of pastoral care. By its very existence, this institution takes what might be only a noble vision and makes it viable in practical day-by-day relationships. People within the congregation know each other, at least to a certain extent. People within the congregation accept some responsibility for mutual help. People within the congregation ought to be able to count on the sympathy and support of other members. Pastoral care becomes the primary agency by which these responsibilities are made effective.

The Holy Spirit in the Parish

Perhaps any such statement of what the Church in history is meant to be, and what the local congregation is meant to make manifest in local situations, has the immediate result of making people conscious of the failure of the Church as a whole and the parish in particular to serve very effectively. The Gospel, however, never claims that unaided men and women can fulfill God's purpose in human affairs—rather the reverse, so that the failure of the Church may at least partially be charged to assumptions of self-sufficiency in the ministry both of the clergy and the members.

Together with an understanding of the pastoral responsibility of the congregation the Christian view of things demands that the Church be understood in the light of the doctrine of the Holy Spirit, particularly as this applies to congregational affairs. God not only uses the Church as his normal instrument, he indwells the Church's life. While the military phrase, *esprit de corps,* does not fully explain what is meant, there is a sense in which it is most apt. The relationship of Christians to each other is not simply that of like-minded people who are associated because of the things they have in common; rather, there is a sense that the fellowship with its ongoing life sustains the members and gives them an identity with each other which they could never create for themselves.

The doctrine of the Holy Spirit applies in basic principle to the Holy Catholic Church, as in the third paragraph of the Apostles' Creed; but its force is felt in the living relationships of men and women within a Christian congregation, and wherever people are willing to trust the Lordship of Christ and the forgiving love of God as they make their daily decisions. It is not the role of the ordained clergy to be exclusive agents through whom the Holy Spirit makes his power felt within the life of the Church, but it is their role to point up dynamically and dramatically the reality and necessity for this power.

The ministry of pastoral care, therefore, is not only a

reflection of the way God is concerned for his children, like a shepherd for his sheep; it is also a manifestation of the power of the Holy Spirit working in the life of the Church. God provides strength through the Church's activities and resources to those who need help. While this is not limited to the duties of the professional clergy, it is most obviously seen in what they do.

The Congregation in the Modern City

While it is true that the ministry of pastoral care is one of the most important ways through which the congregation serves its own members and reaches out to those round about who do not as yet identify themselves with the Christian Church, it ought to be taken into account that the congregation itself is in a major phase of evolution. The change in the nature of congregational life, at this mid-period of the Twentieth Century, at one and the same time adds to the need people may feel for pastoral care and makes its availability that much more difficult.

The congregation, as we know it in American churches, is not only rooted in the ancient Jewish synagogue system, it is also in the medieval village church of northern Europe. In the latter, it was made up of those who lived in small communities and who knew each other and a great deal about each other, whose lives were interlocked socially and economically, and who found their parish church to be the major symbolic-center of their community life. Survivals of this system can be seen in some of the German-American communities of the midwest and southwest, where the congregation-community was transplanted to America, and in many ways still survives after several generations.

The congregation in the modern American city, however, is a different matter. People do not know each other in the same way. Living near to each other does not provide the same basis for community as do vocational relationships, or special interests, or children in the same school. While certain suburban churches in new residential areas show a kind of vital community interest between the members, a number of factors make this a passing phase. The high mobility of population—people are either transferred or just choose to move—continually breaks up the community feeling, and this is reflected in the tone of congregational life. In apartment house areas the problem is much more difficult, and even the established residential neighborhoods are marked by the same kind of failure to know one's neighbors and by an increasing tendency to move from house to house.

This change in the nature of urban life tends to make membership in a particular parish more a matter of accident than anything else. Individuals and families affiliate because: (1) they just drop in and seem to find a welcome; (2) they have heard about the minister as a preacher; (3) they have friends already belonging and they want to go where their friends are; (4) the educational program (possibly with certain social by-products) seems good for their children; and, (5) there are unquestionably appeals of social prestige, even of snob-value. To the extent that these factors become influential, the congregation cannot be assumed to provide the note of family-of-families to those who belong. Even when they go every Sunday, people can be strangers and pilgrims in the household of God.

The idea of God's pastorate of his people becomes difficult to appreciate where the minister or the church staff provides the real common denominator for a number of people who live all over the place, and who overlap other people geographically, people who are socially and culturally akin, and who belong to other churches or even to other parishes of the same communion. This pastorate is projected on the ordained clergy themselves without an appreciation of the context in which they work, thus tending to make their help more like that of the doctor or dentist, or even psychiatrist, than of the person who focuses for them the life of the larger family in which they find real meaning for their own lives.

The fact that the role and self-understanding of the congregation is in a major stage of evolution in no respect changes the way in which the ministry of pastoral care, in the last analysis, depends upon the existence of concrete fellowships representing the Church, in which people identify themselves as they find life's meaning. What it does mean is that Christians cannot assume that pastoral care will be appreciated for what it is meant to be. Parish activities continue much as they have been. The clergy's duties change only gradually. The basic issue is one of recovering a dynamic sense of the *why* of congregational life, expressed in ways which appreciate the realities of modern city life, rather than trying to recapture the flavor of an earlier age. This can make a vital difference to the way people actually live and meet life's problems.

Pastoral Care in Parish and Community

Pastoral care consists of many activities with which all Christians are more or less familiar. The clergy visit the members of their parishes, sometimes using lay associates to help with the task. This kind of across-the-board pastoral visiting is a perpetual reminder, in a low-pressure way, that God is concerned and that the fellowship of God's Holy People, indwelt by the Holy Spirit, is more than a list of names filed alphabetically in a card catalogue.

In the name of the Holy People of God the clergy visit the sick, those in hospitals and institutions, and those who are chronically ill. The clergy prepare parents and god-parents for the sacrament of Holy Baptism so that, when a baby is received into the fellowship of Christ's flock, there is a sense of pastoral responsibility on the part of all concerned. The clergy through premarital conferences involving planning, counseling, required reading and consultations with physicians, prepare young people for marriage in order that this sacrament be not simply a social convention implemented by religio-moral sanctions but an expression of the Church's ongoing life where every family is *ecclesiola in ecclesia,* the little church within the Church.

The clergy minister to the dying and to the families of the bereaved, in order that people may pass through the valley of the shadow in the awareness that they do not walk life's trail alone. They are also available for personal conferences with those in difficulty, in the course of which they may seek to make available in the most cooperative and coordinated manner possible, the resources of medicine, psychiatry, and social case work, by enlisting the help of experts or by referrals to those with special skills.

What pastoral care may consist of in detail obviously will vary according to (a) the ground-rules, so to speak, of the communion in which a clergyman ministers, and (b) the work load which he assumes or finds himself obliged to carry. Yet despite these differences in structure and opportunity, it is assumed in most of the mainstream traditions of western Christendom, Protestant and Catholic, that the ministry of pastoral care is not an extra— something added on the side to an already complete vocational pattern—but that in its way it is just as fundamental to the Christian ministry in the world as preaching the Gospel and administering the sacraments.

Pastoral care, in the form of face-to-face meetings with people, is an essential in the life of every Christian Church which is fulfilling its function, yet it is not automatically effective nor even understood for what it is meant to be. The opportunities for this aspect of the ministry exist wherever people are, since they need to get to know, trust and love each other, and find help and strength through their relationships for dealing with life's normal crises and extraordinary difficulties. But while the responsibilities are there wherever ministers are engaged in professional Christian service, there are also difficulties to be faced.

In a situation where, for example, one minister is trying to serve several mission stations at the same time, his opportunities for personal pastoral relationships may be few—because of the time required to handle the essentials in separated flocks, and because in small communities there is often a reticence about bringing personal matters to someone else's attention. Nevertheless, the opportunities will exist—at least through the ministry to the sick, the counseling necessary before baptisms and marriages, and in the ministry to the bereaved. And even more intimate relationships may well arise when it becomes known that the pastor is concerned and available, and is going to remain in the community long enough to be trusted.

In the reverse situation—that toward which the American parish church seeks to aspire—the gigantic parish with a full program and many activities and multitudinous members, the opportunities for pastoral care appear to be much greater. Yet here they may be interfered with by the fact that the very size of the operation precludes much personal encounter between those who belong and those professionally in charge of affairs. Opportunities for pastoral care certainly arise in the course of the normal ministrations of any parish church. Yet often those who need help

15

do not know that it is available or how to go about asking for it, while the pastor's available time for this aspect of his ministry is taken up by long-term cases—which, while they certainly are also "God's children," are very time-consuming—and by people from the larger community who come in their desperate need, not knowing where else to turn nor what to look for.

The point I am trying to make is simply this: opportunities for pastoral care exist wherever congregational life is found; yet at the same time there is a real danger that those who need the care will be overlooked because of a number of factors which interfere with the minister's recognition of their need, or even knowing they exist as persons, and because people generally are not too clear as to what they may hope to receive through the ministry of pastoral concern. Some larger churches attempt to meet this problem by assigning ministers with special training, aptitude or particular interest to this special duty, and then advertising their availability. This seems to me to accentuate the difficulties just mentioned as much as it attempts to get around them.

Despite the difficulties, however, pastoral care is a necessary function of the Church's life and its ministry to an anxious world. The problems in availability and understanding, and the administrative difficulties in serving those who have the greatest need for help, require us to re-think continually how the ministry may serve its Lord through the pastorate to men and women who are called to be the "children of God," whether or not they appreciate what this relationship makes available to them. A continual re-examination both of ways and means and of basic theology is called for, if the role of pastor is to be of maximum usefulness in the world for which Christ died.

CHAPTER II

PASTORAL CARE
AND THE
DOCTRINE OF THE CHURCH

Pastoral care within the ongoing life of the Christian Church is a reflection of the doctrine of the Holy Spirit in those areas where people seek to meet each other helpfully. Anything done in the way of implementing the Christian faith in the world of daily problems, tensions, and decisions must be a reflection of the doctrine of the Holy Spirit, if it is to be seriously Christian.

The doctrine of the Holy Spirit is the Christian's way of describing his awareness that God's love is already at work in and through the relationships men have with each other in the world. While people may not recognize this reality as being part of the world's normal economic, political, and social life, the Christian conviction is that God uses the plans and purposes of men in his divine scheme with or without their conscious cooperation and even when they think of themselves as deliberately opposed to Christian principles.

The Holy Spirit is at work in the Church in the same way as in all human enterprise, but with this radical difference. The Church is conscious of its responsibility to be the agency of God's loving concern for people, whereas other human institutions and activities may usually be indifferent to this. The Church exists because the Christian faith binds men and women together in loyal response to God's saving gift of Jesus Christ and his continuing saving action in history and his ultimate victory beyond the end of time.

The Church exists because of the Christian faith; yet, at the same time, it is the normal instrument through which men discover the faith and it is also the framework within which they live it. The Christian faith is discovered, appreciated and lived as a person finds himself belonging to that fellowship of men and women who dare to call themselves the Body of Christ.

There are many titles which have been given the Church —the Fellowship of the Resurrection, that group called into being through the power of the risen Christ, in order to reflect him both to its own members and to the world; the Extension of the Incarnation, that group which carries on in its own way in history the redemptive mission begun by our Lord; the Spirit-Inspired Fellowship, that group through which God makes himself known through continually opening new windows of the soul as men and women are led to see the relevance of the faith in the circumstances of a changing world. The Church claims to be the one unique fellowship in which people are organically connected with each other, yet at the same time individually free. The Church claims to be the true home within history for those who are otherwise strangers and pilgrims. Yet the Church always points beyond itself to a higher loyalty and a home beyond history. As St. Paul said in the Epistle to the Philippians, "We are a *politeuma* of heaven"—a colony which seeks to reflect here a basis of life which could never be developed by itself.

The Church is of its nature missionary, and its mission applies to those who are already technically connected in order that they may become more deeply convinced and seriously committed as well as to those whose connection with the Christian tradition is either tenuous or nonexistent. The Church has to be missionary or cease to be itself, because its underlying purpose is to provide men in historical circumstances with the one relationship in which they can be truly themselves, daring to accept their sinful selves as worth God's love. Thus they are enabled to find a way of living with anxiety, fear, and loneliness which does not destroy personhood in the course of relieving pain.

The Christian Church, as the beloved community of God's faithful people, exists as the manifestation in time and space of God's saving action in Jesus Christ, our Lord. This involves an inward appreciation of the Resurrection as this is put in the second collect for Easter Day: *Grant us so to die daily from sin, that we may evermore live with him . . .* And it simultaneously involves a confidence that grace and forgiveness are not just once-and-for-all discoveries, but rather that they are continually rediscovered as people meet each other in all sorts of practical situations.

The Christian Church by its very existence, therefore, maintains that God's normative way of mediating saving love to men and women is in, and through, a relationship which they have with each other in conscious loyalty to Christ, the Lord. This is not a static but a dynamic relationship in which people, as they seek to deal with life's daily demands, are at the same time inspired to re-interpret for each other the sufficiency of the saving Christ in a changing world.

The doctrine of the Holy Spirit makes clear to us that God uses you to sustain my faith and to communicate to me over and over again the fact that I am accepted and forgiven through the love of Christ, and that God uses me to communicate this same saving reality over and over again to you. The doctrine of the Holy Spirit is the way the Christian Church describes the fact that God seeks to use the meetings people have with each other at home, and in business, and everywhere else, as occasions for imparting the dynamic of redemptive love to a confused and tragic world. On the one side of the coin, so to speak, is the reality that we need each other to be ourselves, and on the other side is the saying of our Lord, *Where two or three are gathered together in my name.*

The Tragedy of the Human Situation

It is one thing to talk about human relationships in the presence of Christ and under the inspiration of the Holy Spirit; it is quite another thing to recognize the realities of individual and social life for what they are. From the outset biblical religion has been: (1) a proclamation of what the divine purpose expects of man in every area of life—private, family, work, community, national, etc.; (2) the pronouncement of the divine judgment on a world which does not respond to its opportunities in line with the divine purpose, because the fears and anxieties of sinful men and groups lead to separation and bitterness and distrust; and, (3) the announcement in all confidence and courage that God in Christ Jesus has taken the initiative in bringing about a reconciliation. Yet the fact remains that men do not appreciate answers to questions they do not understand themselves to be asking.

Pastoral care is perhaps best seen as an aspect of God's reconciling love in action, expressed through the concern of human beings seeking to speak to each other in the presence of Christ. Yet, before pastoral care can become effective, the other two steps have to be appreciated; there is a divine perspective in which alone men and women can truly be themselves as they were meant to be. While this cannot be reduced to a simple formula which prevents problems from arising, it can be appreciated as the framework within which we face our problems; and there is a divine judgment on human pretensions to be self-sufficient and to live in a man-centered universe. The facts of daily life, wherever we turn to observe it, deny the kind of pattern which our faith in Christ suggests that God intends for all his children. Men and women, as individuals and in social groups, are so often tragically at cross-purposes with themselves and with their world when it comes to meeting what life seems to demand of them. Within this context, however, pastoral care can humbly yet responsibly reflect the divine love seeking the lost.

Without going into a detailed analysis of breakdown in individual and social affairs, we can see that there is a tremendous need for what the doctrine of the Church stands for. At one and the same time people are more interdependent in all sorts of ways than ever before in the world's history; and they are also more cut off from fulfilling relationships with each other than apparently was ever true in earlier ages. Regardless of other factors which may accentuate the problem here and there, the very size of economic, political, and social operations in the mid-period of the Twentieth Century makes the individual personalities involved seem small and insignificant.

The size of modern cities and the influence of the large-city attitude even in smaller communities make it more

21

difficult for people really to meet as persons, although they are neighbors sociologically. At the same time the mobility of great segments of that part of the population with more educational and cultural advantages adds to the problem of people relating to each other. When, every so often, individuals and families are plucked up by the roots, so to speak, they tend more and more to avoid getting involved with their new neighbors, because the process of separation is painful.

Again, a large part of business and industry attains its efficiency through mass production methods with the result that goods and services are made more cheaply available to a wide public; but the price of this efficiency is often turning people into interchangeable parts and adjuncts to the machines they serve. In other words, people tend less and less to meet their co-workers as partners in a significant enterprise. The trades unions were never officially meant to solve this problem, yet the title "Brotherhood" in some industries suggests that this issue was once felt to be important. In most of the larger industries unions are too big and impersonal, even in the locals, to serve this purpose; and indeed one of the major causes of corruption in the unions is the fact that men have not learned to live together as partners in activities involving many people. Outside of the factories, most employed people do not even have the theoretical partnership of industrial associations, and therefore they have no means, other than those they make for themselves, of meeting other people as persons.

When people find it difficult to have meaningful relationships with others in the communities where they live and in the enterprises where they work, they tend to take home with them the same sense of isolation, with the result that separatedness becomes reflected in the family too.

Husbands and wives find it difficult to communicate with each other and with their children, if this is the only area in which truly interpersonal relationships are possible. While the family at its best will, of course, provide for more intimate meetings than any other association, it usually cannot carry the ball alone and provide for interpersonal fulfillment in a world which otherwise denies it.

Yet people have to meet in the course of getting the world's work done and in taking care of themselves and their responsibilities. The very fact that this is the case brings home to sensitive souls the problem of loneliness, even in the midst of crowds, which the Church seeks to overcome in the name of Christ. The doctrine of the Holy Spirit makes clear to us that since we need each other to be ourselves, God uses the meeting of people as the occasion for imparting the dynamic of love to a confused and tragic world.

In one important sense, the doctrine of the Holy Spirit suggests that God's loving purpose is in direct conflict with the "spirits" of the times. The Holy Spirit is not the only dynamic influence organizing people in fellowship and purporting to give them a direction for life. Every meeting, whether of one person with another or of people in groups, is under the influence of some kind of spirit. St. Paul's imagery of *principalities and powers* and *the rulers of the darkness of this world* applies not only to the interpretation of the social and psychic forces which he saw operative in his day, but quite as much to this twentieth-century world, even though we may use a different terminology to describe what is going on. Just as teenage boys on Hallowe'en can reveal a destructive spirit as they tear around together, so the world is marked by destructive "spirits." We do not need to think of the Nazis or of world Communism to see this fact. It is equally manifest in "white supremacy movements" in this country and in all other socially destructive movements.

The doctrine of the Holy Spirit is the Christian's way of describing his conviction that God's loving purpose takes the offensive against the destructive spirits of our times, and that the ultimate victory is in the Lord's hands. The doctrine of the Holy Spirit is the Christian conviction, sustained in the life of the Christian community generation after generation—even though often played down and sometimes partially forgotten—that when our loyalty to Christ is the determinative factor in our meetings with each other, then God's influence can overcome the spirits of discord and destruction and lead us to discover redemptive possibilities in all kinds of situations.

The Christian Church in this sense is the fellowship of the Holy Spirit seeking to make it possible for people to discover that all sorts of meetings of real people, who have to deal with real concerns, are at the same time earnests of God's saving action in history. Christian doctrine can have no vital meaning until it is seen to be reflected in the problem areas of human life, but when there is serious prayer and work to bring this about, we can understand in our hearts what St. John's Gospel says, *When the Comforter is come, whom I will send unto you from the Father, even the Spirit of truth, which proceedeth from the Father, he shall testify of me: and ye also shall bear witness . . .*

Pastoral Care in the Church

Pastoral care is that activity of the Church's life—largely but not exclusively carried on by the clergy—which seeks to make *explicit* in particular meetings between people, in the presence of the saving Christ, what is meant to be *implicit* in all meetings. It is in this sense that pastoral care is a reflection of the doctrine of the Holy Spirit inspiring the Church of Christ. Indeed it is meant to make this doctrine concrete, as those charged with pastoral responsibilities seek to mediate God's acceptance, forgiveness, and love to specific problem situations in which individuals, families, and groups find themselves prisoners of their own anxieties and frustrations.

All Christian pastoral work occurs within the context of the doctrine of the Church, where the most that can be attempted in practical problem situations is to demonstrate that we can dare to see in ourselves persons for whom Christ died, and persons in and through whom Christ seeks to live. Likewise this is the value of the persons with whom we are dealing. In other words, pastoral care rests upon the conviction that God will use this meeting of persons, where people are being helped to live with themselves in reality, as a dynamic manifestation of the Church as the beloved community of God's Holy People. Pastoral care depends upon a deeply-held and appreciated conviction that it is only within the Spirit-inspired fellowship that selfhood can be accepted as other than a problem, so that when two or more selves meet in this context grace and forgiveness can be shared.

Without a sharp awareness of the context of the doctrine of the Church, pastoral care tends to become a more or less specialized rendering of assistance to people in trouble, with nothing to distinguish it, except for a kind of amateur status, from the services supplied by community resources—psychiatry, social agencies, marriage counseling bureaus, and the like. With a sharp awareness of the significance of the Holy Spirit, pastoral care becomes not a substitute for necessary specialized skills, but rather the indispensable communication to troubled souls of the saving framework in which profound healing takes place, whether primarily through the help of the pastor or through his cooperation with those who supply technical specialties for dealing with human distress.

In the Episcopal Church and in many other communions, both Protestant and Catholic, the service of the Holy Communion is the liturgical way by which the connection between the doctrine of the Church and the ministry of pastoral care are both dramatized and communicated effectively to the worshippers. Those who come bring themselves as they are with all their worries and fears and unsolved problems, and they dare to come because they know that within the fellowship of God's Holy People they are wanted for who they are—God's children—in spite of all their failures and conflicts. They offer themselves (the only thing they have to offer in the last analysis) and receive themselves back at the altar rail, cleansed, forgiven, loved, and commissioned. Then they leave the church building to go back into the world as *themselves,* the Church, bearing the saving love of Christ into every area into which their daily routines and special responsibilities carry them. The priest has the same need as the communicant in the pew, makes the same offering and receives the same gift and commission. The psychiatrist, the social worker, and the medical doctor can each offer his essential human self and his professional skill within the same liturgical act.

Pastoral Care and Other Disciplines

It goes without saying that pastoral care is only one aspect of the Church's life in the world and only one of the means through which the Church, as the instrumentality of the Holy Spirit, seeks to confront the world with the saving power of Christ as relevant to all men everywhere, in all situations in every age. Certainly the doctrine of the Holy Spirit includes an understanding that no political, economic, sociological or technological development will ever make the Christian faith irrelevant, but rather that concerned Christians will be able to discover how the Gospel may speak effectively even to an interplanetary age. Therefore, pastoral care must take its place in cooperation with the priestly and prophetic ministries of the same fellowship in the never-ending task of mediating God's saving love to those who were born to be his children in a world where social change is real, "new occasions teach new duties," and God provides many resources to be teamed together in his name.

Pastoral care, in the sense of the ministry of the Church to individuals and to small groups, is certainly not the only way the Church is meant to operate in history; but, on the other hand, no interpretation of the Church's mission to the world can be regarded as adequate if the pastoral ministry is not seriously coordinated with the priestly and prophetic—not merely as an application of what is derived elsewhere to certain *ad hoc* situations to which attention must be given, but rather as an indispensable means of communicating God's grace and forgiveness to troubled persons. Indeed, unless the ministry of pastoral care connects Christian faith and life to specific situations, the whole Christian scheme tends to become abstract and unimportant for very many people.

Pastoral care is also coordinate with theology—systematic, apologetic, and moral. Theology in its traditional claim to be "Queen of the Sciences" is meant to be that area of human understanding in which the various intellectual disciplines find their common center. True as this may be in theory, it tends to remain abstract until those disciplines which bear upon the lives of persons and the development of society are able to find a practical as well as a theoretical center in being dedicated to the service of him who is Lord both of those who serve and of those being served.

Such a meeting of the psychological, social, and therapeutic sciences under the influence of the Holy Spirit does not imply any denial of the integrity of the discipline concerned in the area of its particular competence; and it certainly does not suggest that the cure of souls can be a substitute for psychotherapy or social case work or other specialized counseling services where these are called for, nor to take the place of social psychology and specialized group work where these are germane. Rather it suggests, first of all, that those who take responsibility for mediating God's concern for his children within the life of the Church have the responsibility of being as conversant as possible with these skills which, in the last analysis, must be understood, theologically, to be gifts of God and of the order of Creation. It suggests further that the doctrine of the Holy Spirit may be seen to be operative when the pastoral ministry enables those with special skills to cooperate effectively with each other and with the patient-client as fellow members of God's Holy People. Unless those charged with pastoral responsibility, however, evidence their understanding and respect for special disciplines in the areas of their particular competence, such a coordination of what God has made available in the fullest possible service to his children remains a pious hope.

The Church is obviously not the only institution in modern society seeking to help individuals deal with their problems and to influence social directions, but the Church can serve as the rallying center for services on the part of some of God's children to others who need help, provided that the Church seeks to bring these disciplines into contact with the doctrine of the Holy Spirit—not as a concept but as a saving force in the world. The Church respects special skills for what they are and proclaims to the world that all men and all institutions, including therapists and group workers as well as those they serve, stand in need of God's grace and forgiveness, as do also those represent-ing the Church's life in responsibility for pastoral care.

The Christian faith does not make unnecessary the use of special scientific services for people in trouble, but rather makes possible a heightened appreciation of what serious studies and disciplines may provide. The Christian faith should make it possible for Christians to recognize that sometimes the Holy Spirit seems to communicate saving truth more effectively through secular programs than through those with an official ecclesiastical connection. But the Christian Church is primarily interested in making it possible for people to meet consciously as members of the Holy People of God, those rendering service quite as much as those to whom it is supplied, because it is Chris-tian conviction that only within this framework of shared life can the fullest possibilities of the therapeutic, educa-tional, and group development services be realized. The ministry of pastoral care has among its functions the task of making this concrete.

Pastoral Care as a Relationship

The pastoral ministry is primarily a relationship between those who have been called to a special role within the household of faith and those who belong quite as much to the Holy People of God as do the clergy, yet who have special needs requiring skillful attention. This is true whether or not the people concerned know or feel them-selves to belong to the fellowship. It is God's purpose that they be found, and that they find themselves in the process. The common denominator of counselor and counselee is something more important than that they both belong to the human race. It must be expressed in the words of the first epistle of Peter, *But ye are a chosen generation, a royal priesthood, an holy nation, a peculiar people; that ye should shew forth the praises of him who hath called you out of darkness into his marvelous light: Which in time past were not a people, but are now the people of God . . .*

Pastoral care is one aspect of the life of the Christian fellowship. It involves the more or less specialized service of some members on behalf of other members. But the relationship of the pastor and the people with whom he counsels depends upon both belonging to the fellowship, so that in an ultimate sense their dependency is upon God and not upon each other. In practical matters it is often necessary for people to use the special training and talents of other people to solve immediate problems. In this sense the relationship between the pastor and those with whom he works is not unlike that of a dentist or a plumber, an automobile or television repair man, or a psychiatrist: he is straightening out a problem brought to him for attention. But unlike all other forms of human service, the pastoral relationship is dependent upon a dominant, functional relationship which in the other cases might exist, but is not a prerequisite for effective service.

Pastoral care, therefore, in the technical meaning of the term, refers to those relationships between the various ministries of the Church and individuals or families where the end in view is to help the people involved to live more effectively with themselves in the presence of God and in the company of God's people. The occasions for this type of relationship arise out of the dislocations which can so easily occur in the normal course of living—physical illness, emotional distress, the death of loved ones, problems with children, heavy responsibilities, job changes, financial difficulties, etc. In any of these situations the Church may be, even though it isn't always, the most easily available resource to which people who are confused about the meaning of their predicament may turn for help. Likewise many of these situations involve the acceptance of responsibility by those in the official ministry of the Church to take the initiative at least where their own parishioners are concerned. That is, we do not have to be asked to make a sick call; we call because someone is sick.

Pastoral care may be limited simply to the relationships between the pastor and the people who need his help, or it may involve tripartite or multilateral contacts where a variety of resources is being used to help meet the problem. The important thing about pastoral care in this description is that, regardless of what insight the parishioner may have into his own problem or into the theological meaning of the Church, he feels nevertheless that he may by right claim the concerned attention of the fellowship to which he belongs. Furthermore, a great many people without any particular church association, indeed without any particular religious convictions, feel that they may call upon any convenient minister to take an interest in their problems without any prior basis for the relationship, and that they should find a welcome when they come.

Through the ministry of pastoral concern, therefore, the doctrine of the Church as the Holy People of God becomes a living and healing reality in a world where so often there is such a cleavage between what ought to be and what is. Every aspect of congregational life, and every service performed both by the professional clergy and lay volunteers, is meant to be a reflection of the doctrine of the Church, in concrete terms in practical situations.

CHAPTER III

PASTORAL CARE AND
THE SELF-UNDERSTANDING
OF THE MINISTER

As church life and organization have developed in the Twentieth Century, the ordained minister has come to be regarded as the primary agent through whom the Christian fellowship fulfills its responsibility for pastoral care. While some branches of Protestantism in America have lay deacons and deaconesses theoretically set apart for this work, these at best tend to become aids to the pastor, or helpers, rather than full and equal sharers of a common ministry. There is no question about the fact that the ordained clergy have as one of their official functions the task of seeing that pastoral care is provided; but it is quite another thing for them to think of themselves as having exclusive authority over this aspect of the Church's life because this tends to identify the Church with the clergy and to make the laity not really participants in a fellowship, but rather the objects of its concern.

At the same time that we recognize the continual temptation of both clergymen and laymen to act as if the ordained ministry constituted the Church in a way which the laymen do not share, we also recognize that, since the earliest days, the Church has had need of an ordained, officially set-apart ministry. It is not within the province of this book to deal with the origin and development of Church order as such, but recognition must be given to the fact that the ministry has always had a necessary part to play in the Church's ongoing life. There have been many theological interpretations given as to what this means, and these concepts have been reflected in differing policies and practices. The fact remains, however, that in no area is confusion of thought and feelings, as well as action, greater than in that of pastoral care.

From the earliest days of the Christian movement, it has been understood as necessary for the Church's life and health that certain persons be set aside to give a major part of their time, energy, and interest to concern for those who needed care. Without taking the story in the sixth chapter of the Book of the Acts—of the selecting of the seven deacons—to be a literal account of the institution of that office in the Christian tradition, we can recognize that even as early as apostolic times, the Church felt that provision had to be made for the exercise of pastoral responsibility along with the preaching of the Word and "the breaking of bread."

It is interesting to realize that provision for the pastorate was made at least as early as systematic provision for the priesthood and for preaching. The apostolic Church, which was still in a very formative period in Church order, understood that it had to make some official arrangements for the care of the lonely and the poor and the sick and the bereaved. From the outset the Christian fellowship has taken seriously our Lord's statement: *Inasmuch as ye have done it unto one of the least of these my brethren, ye have done it unto me,* and it has delegated responsibility to its official ministry for fulfilling this injunction.

In the biblical understanding of pastoral responsibility, Christian concern has never been meant to be something restricted to the clergy, but rather they have been charged with the task of helping the congregation as a whole fulfill its pastoral charge. What has developed, however, is a situation in which those who have been ordained are charged with representatively—on behalf of the fellowship—taking practical steps toward carrying out what is in principle everybody's responsibility. Since the old adage, "What is everybody's business is nobody's business," is true in practice, it is obviously the duty of those who are giving full-time service to the Church's life and work to see to it that the work is done. But it does not follow from this that the duties, and with them the privilege and authority of being able to give and to withhold services, should become means through which men in the ordained ministry justify to themselves what they are doing.

While the ways and means through which the ministry of pastoral care have been carried on have varied down through the centuries, it has generally been understood that this function is important to the Church being itself. When the pastoral side of the Church's life has seemed to be neglected, special movements have arisen to see that it was provided. If these movements, such as some of the charitable religious orders of the Middle Ages, could find a place in official Christendom, well and good; but if not, the work went on anyhow under semi-official or unofficial auspices.

Many of the special ministries to human need—social, psychological, economic, medical—which the modern community provides are the result of the failure of the clergy, as leaders of the Church, to take adequate steps to see that there was a vital response to the call of human suffering, and of the equally important fact that the complexity of modern society demands more skills than any class of individuals can hope to provide within itself. Nevertheless, the fact remains that modern social case work, hospital administration, and many other community services are reflections of the original delegation to the Church and its ministry of care for the total personalities, not only for the souls, of those for whom the Church has concern. While the task of ministering to the multifarious needs of modern men in the modern world has become subdivided into many important and useful specialties, the original assignment of concern for people as persons is still the responsibility of the clergy.

While there has been an evolution and development in the number and nature of the resources available to help people in the modern community, so that the ministry does not have to carry the full load alone, there has at the same time been an evolution of the duties which the clergy themselves are expected to carry. The village church of medieval Europe, and even of Reformation times, where the minister could know everybody, and with a minimum of help could see to the maintenance of a simple parish life, has given way to the church in the modern city where, regardless of the size of the particular parish, there are many sides of congregational life where the minister has some responsibility.

Pastoral care becomes one of a number of duties carried by men who are in the ministry. The same man in most instances is not only a pastor but serves a number of other roles at the same time. This is both an advantage and a liability. It is an advantage to the extent that the clergyman concerned both knows and feels that his various functions are all in some significant way representative of the Church in history. It is a liability to the extent that these functions compete with each other for the man's time, energy, and interest, and this is often very frustrating. Yet it is important to remember that the pastor is not a person by himself. He is the same person who is priest and prophet.

While we live in an age of specialization, which is at least partly the result of techniques demanding such extensive special training that it is impossible for anyone to be master of very many specialties, the fact remains that the Christian ministry is still a derivative of the Church. No matter how competent a clergyman may become in some particular phase of his ministry, what he does is still an implementation in a particular area of the same doctrine of the Church which applies to all other areas affected by the ministry.

There has been an unfortunate tradition dividing the functions of the ministry between prophet, priest and pastor, and the modern world has added the functions of administrator and educator (and in some instances the additional functions of engineer and public relations man!). The division seems to suggest that if a man is gifted in one of these functions, or assigned particularly to one of these responsibilities, he is not meant to be over-involved in the others. The reports of a number of studies which have been made about the problems of emotional breakdown in the ministry seem to suggest that at least a major contributory cause is the conflict in the heart of a man who finds himself serving diverse functions which often appear to get in each other's way.

The Pastor's Image of Himself

Clergymen, like everyone else, try to describe to themselves what they are doing by referring to an image. Where different functions appear to compete with each other, this image is blurred so that a man is unclear as to what it is supposed to be. In the case of the ministry, as in the case of a number of other public service vocations, a further complication exists in the fact that there are also conflicts in what people expect the minister to be. Along with the blurred image a parson may have of himself, therefore, is another blur in the image which he understands others to have of him.

This question of the image, both as a clergyman thinks of his own role and as he takes into account what others may think of him, has a tremendous bearing upon the nature of the pastoral work he finds himself able to do. Ministers who have had clinical training have been confronted with this problem and in many cases have been encouraged to find psychiatric assistance themselves in order to enable them to live with it. This is all to the good. But the theological aspects of the problem are often neglected in favor of the psychological aspects. And insight, as important as it is, is not a substitute for grace.

For instance, there may be a conflict between what the pastor may feel, because he is a man with the instincts and drives of human nature, and what he thinks he ought to be feeling or not feeling because of his clerical role. The pastor may try to be as accepting and understanding as possible but finds that his own emotional needs—either attraction to or repulsion by the personality with whom he is trying to work—may interfere with what he is doing. As he becomes aware of this, he tends to feel guilty for being more concerned with those to whom he is drawn, for one reason or another, and somewhat more cursory in his dealings with those who are less attractive. Since the image he has of his own role tells him that he ought as far as possible to be completely disinterested in his concern for all the children of God, he tends to feel guilty when he realizes that this is not the case. While this is only one example of the kind of conflict which may exist in this area, it will perhaps suggest that those who undertake the ministry of pastoral care may themselves need pastoral help toward fulfilling their role.

Another conflict which blurs the image is in the pastor's own desire to be accepting and understanding of those who come to him for counsel, regardless of where the chips may fall, and his experience that the counselee may find it difficult to articulate what is really on his mind for fear that the counselor will be shocked. This is because people in western society have built up a kind of image of the minister as "the man of God," who is not involved in the ordinary tensions which disturb the average human soul. Although he himself knows this to be untrue, he may encounter some difficulty in helping the counselee get past this blocking image. While the counselee comes to him because he feels that he can count on sympathetic treatment, nothing very much can happen unless the relationship can move beyond the discussion of superficial problems to where the shoe really pinches.

A psychotherapist has described the problem many ministers face in words which, while they are addressed to the confusions attendant to his counseling function, apply to his total operation:

The whole question of role is a disease in modern life, not peculiar to the minister as counselor. The disease consists in the idea that we ought to *know* in advance how to behave in a given situation just the way an actor knows when he starts his evening performance. We think that there is or should be a role of father, mother, doctor, teacher, etc., which we should assume in order to be a good father, mother, doctor, teacher. If we study the distrust of spontaneous behavior which is implicit in this ideal, we can gradually become less in need of playing a role.[1]

An adequate understanding of the doctrine of the Holy Spirit and the theology of the Church could not detach the ministry from the body of the faithful by ascribing a kind of holiness and moral superiority to a special group of people which is not meant at the same time to apply in exactly the same way to everyone else. The Church is the Body of Christ in the world and the ministry is derived from the priestly-prophetic-pastoral nature of the fellowship as a whole. If the ordained ministry of the Church can help members generally to understand that there is a ministry of bookkeeping and a ministry of running homes and a ministry of engineering, then people will be helped to make use of the special services of those competent to render them without some distorting image of the role confusing the picture.

Whether we are looking at the problem of this image of the clergyman's role from his own point of view or from that of what other people expect of him, the fact remains that the image of the clergyman can have no significant meaning except as a reflection of the doctrine of the Church; and a great deal of the confusion of our day, in the minds of the clergy and in the minds of those with whom they work, is a result of detaching the problem of determining the image of the parson from the theology of the Church.

This analysis of the problem of conflicting images would suggest that it is important to appreciate what the Church

[1] Dr. Margaret J. Rioch, "Three Questions in Pastoral Counseling," *Journal of Pastoral Care*, Vol. xiv, No. 2, pp. 104-107; Summer 1960.

really is and what purposes it serves before dealing with the ministry. Yet, when there is some clearer understanding of what the nature of the Church is, the roles of priest, prophet, and pastor, instead of being in destructive conflict, will complement each other. The newer functions which the needs of the modern world have passed to the professional ministry—educator and administrator, for example—would likewise fit into the same general understanding.

It is obviously true that aptitudes differ, and it is also true that the more involved the program of a particular congregation becomes the greater need there may be for specialization within it. It is certainly just as true of the Lord's work, as of any phase of human endeavor, that not everybody can do everything equally well or at the same time, and therefore within the Church there is room for those who give primary attention to preaching or to pastoral counseling or parish administration or to the conduct of public worship and the ministration of the sacraments. Yet when all is said and done, the fact remains that all of these functions derive their significance from the doctrine of the Church. If the doctrine of the Church as the Holy People of God is watered down or not felt very deeply, then these functions do appear to be in conflict with each other as far as the lives of clergymen are concerned; and their diversity certainly confuses the lay parishioner.

The Roles of the Minister

The role of the *priest* is primarily sacramental, symbolically representing the self-offering of the congregation through Christ to God and, in turn, conveying the symbols of God's continuing grace to those who worship. Yet the priest becomes merely a kind of disembodied functionary with reference to the real needs of those whom he serves, if he is not also a pastor. One of the values of the Sacrament of Penance is that it does synthesize the priestly and pastoral roles.[2]

The role of the *prophet*—the preacher—is to present not his own judgment but God's judgment, as best he can interpret it, in the light of scripture and the Church's history upon individual and social conditions which seem to deny God's right to rule. The role of the prophet is always to convict of sin and to point the way to repentance. But, unless he is also a pastor as well, the prophet becomes either a scold or a dispenser of mild moral pep talks. This would mean that in his analysis of the world's predicament in the light of God's judgment, he is also concerned with the people who, as individuals and in groups, are caught in the same predicament.

The role of the *educator* is to provide ways and means by which the funded experience of the Church through the ages is made available for the guidance of people in the contemporary situation. The role of the *administrator* is to see to it that the Christian institution runs as smoothly as possible, not as an end in itself but that the other tasks may be accomplished most effectively.

In the light of all this, the role of the *pastor* is to work specifically with those who need help in living with themselves and with others in the confusions and pressures of modern society. Since the pastor is also priest, prophet, educator and administrator, he cannot help but find some use for his capacity in these other areas in his service to individuals whom he is trying to help to live creatively within the household of faith.

[2] The Sacrament of Penance will be discussed on page 79.

The Ministry to Man's Normality

It is most important in drawing this picture of the minister as pastor to remember that pastoral care is more than therapeutic. The pastor is concerned certainly with the more obvious needs of people for various kinds of help, but he is also concerned for their well-being. The pastoral relationship derives its significance for the special ministries to those in distress from the fact that it is a continuing ministry to life's normality. Unlike the physician, psychiatrist, and social worker who have no professional relationship at all except there be distress of some kind for which their services are needed, the pastor's relationship is just as important when there are no problems crying out for immediate attention.

Because the pastor is necessarily concerned with life's normality, where he has a chance to share in the joys and sorrows of people's everyday living, it follows that the parish is the normal setting for the ministry of pastoral care. While there is indeed occasion for specialized services within the Christian Church, these tend to become spiritually attenuated to the extent that they are removed from normal congregational relationships. In the Anglican Church there is a tradition, which is not always carried out, that every priest needs to be attached to an altar— meaning that every clergyman must function in practical connection with the focus of the religious life of a congregation of normal people, so that what he does in his special assignments is seen as an extension of, rather than a substitute for, his regular ministry among ordinary people.

In his ministry to man's normality, the clergyman is himself continually reminded that there is a distinction between sickness and health, and that it is his task to serve as an agency of spiritual healing. In most instances, he will have many normal and routine parish contacts with the individuals and families of his congregation over and above his special meetings with them to provide guidance, and this will help to keep his understanding of his own ministry in focus. At the same time, his work will serve to remind people that the normal setting for the Christian life is the family of God's children, because as a representative of God's loving concern he is as much interested in their successes and their joys as he is in their defeats and their disappointments.

Behind all the activities which are carried on in modern church life there is meant to be this kind of concern of the minister with those for whose care he is responsible; not as if the minister himself were important as an individual, but rather that his concern is a reflection of God's concern and a primary way through which God expresses his loving care. The educational program, for instance, rests upon the conviction that people need to grow in knowledge and insight as well as in their search for understanding that they are part of a beloved family, and therefore as they grow in knowledge they also grow in grace. Behind the various organizations which play so large a part in the program of many churches must be likewise a conviction that not only is the friendly meeting of people important, and not only are acts of social service to be encouraged, but that both meetings and service find their rationale as extensions of the pastoral ministry.

All of these aspects of the ministry in operation are what is meant by pastoral care, but they can only be understood against the background of God's concern for all his children and the Holy Spirit as effective in the fellowship life of the men and women for whom Christ is Lord.

CHAPTER IV

WHY DO PEOPLE
TURN TO THE CHURCH
FOR HELP?

Pastoral care is a primary function of the Church's life, and even though people may be quite vague as to what it consists of and why it is available, many of them feel that the Church is the most approachable resource to which to turn when they are in trouble. Probably the majority of people, if there were a way to determine relative numbers, are unaware that pastoral care is an available resource; but even though this may be true, it is also true that many men and women seek out the clergy when they want help.

Lonely, isolated persons, without meaningful relationships with other persons whom they feel they can trust deeply, and by whom they are confident they will be accepted, sometimes turn to the Church as drowning people grasp for straws—as a last hope that they will be treated as persons in an impersonal world. Whether or not they have any ideas or even misconceptions about what the Church supplies, or whether or not they wish to talk face-to-face with the clergy or just to take sanctuary under the roof, they come because they want help in living with themselves and with other people in a world of guilt, conflicts, misunderstandings, and pressures.

Why do people turn to the Church? Certainly no simple answer can be given. In any downtown church where the doors are open, men and women stop by from early morning till late at night, usually not to see anybody but for a few moments of prayer or quiet meditation. The fact that people feel that the Church is available to them provides the framework in which they may consult the clergy or other counseling resources when they want to. In any event, many people feel, though usually in a rather vague way, that religious institutions provide an undergirding for their lives, a reminder that God's love can be a factor in the handling of their problems.

Probably two basic motivations influence people who turn to the Church. The first is the ancient tradition of sanctuary, older than Christianity but woven definitely into the Christian scheme of things during the Middle Ages. The Church is the symbol of safety in the sense that no matter how inadequate or unworthy or defeated a person may feel himself to be, here is the refuge which is his for the taking.

The second motivation is the feeling that the Church exists to provide concerned attention for all who feel the need for it. While many people will be apologetic when they ask such attention, they still ask. Others feel little hesitation in barging in to demand. While in downtown churches this may often take the form of requests for financial assistance, it would be a mistake to think that this is the real context for the relationship. Rather, people tend to feel that the Church and its staff are maintained in order to be available when needed.

Behind many approaches to the Church for pastoral care of one kind or another are the more or less dimly remembered, and inaccurately understood, experiences of religious training. Regardless of the terms people use in this area, they are saying to themselves that somehow or other through the Church they can find a sustaining confidence, or they ought to be able to find such a confidence. Therefore, when some people feel depressed or confused and uncertain, they may feel that the very existence of the Church should provide the corrective, usually described as "faith."

Sometimes people come seeking a faith they never really had, but it would be inaccurate and unfair to make too much of this. Probably equally as often they come feeling that in some way they can return to the certainties and securities of childhood so that the existence of the Church becomes a kind of projection of idealized parental support.

Again, some people come to the Church looking for punishment in order that they may be able to unload the guilt which oppresses them. They do not so much expect help which will heal their disturbed personalities, as they hope to receive some kind of spiritual spanking for their real or imagined breaches of what they take to be God's law. The Church, understood to be a sanction of moral law and order, is expected to rebuke the offender and, in so doing, make him feel that he has atoned in some manner. He does not very often expect that the minister whom he consults will help him re-think his whole self-understanding in order that moral development will have a new context, only that he will be punished and turned loose again.

In many instances, people turn to the Church because somehow they have heard that they can speak in confidence without fear of betrayal. The ancient tradition of the "sanctity of the confessional" has been extended to the pastor's study, even though those who come are sensible of this rather than confident of it. In many situations, they feel it necessary to raise the question of whether they may speak in confidence, and to be reassured that this is the case; yet the very fact that the question arises suggests that there is both a need for a confidential relationship with another person and a tradition that the Church somehow makes this available.

Very few people who turn to the Church for pastoral help have any real appreciation of the meaning of the Church as the Holy People of God or of the clergy as persons through whom the concern of the family of God's people for its members is expressed. Yet, on the other hand, there is not so real a gulf as might appear between what people are looking for and the basis on which the Church tries to meet them, because basic to whatever problem brings a person into the Church is a feeling of loneliness and the hope that somehow his separation from God and from other people may be overcome. He may not use these words but this is what he feels.

Trouble Isolates People

When men and women are in any sort of trouble, they tend to concentrate on whatever is bothering them. In direct proportion to what they feel to be its seriousness or its pressure, this difficulty, whatever it is, tends to crowd out other considerations. While in a great many situations people can go ahead and do their daily work and give it the attention it demands, the awareness of their personal problems intrudes into consciousness whenever there is a respite from the normal demands of the task. This awareness also limits the use of imagination and energy beyond the routine to which people are accustomed.

Whether we are concerned with physical illness, emotional distress, economic pressure, or worry over the prob-

47

lems of those close to us, or any of the other difficulties which, when they occur, tend to take over in our lives, the very existence of these problems has the effect of cutting us off, more or less, from a feeling of participation in and support by the fellowship of the People of God. In other words, our pains, our worries, and our fears tend to circumscribe our individual universes; and to the degree we feel them to be serious, they make us consider our other interests and responsibilities in their light. A person feels alone almost in direct proportion to the extent of the internal or external pressure to which he may feel himself to be subject.

The curse of most problems of the spirit is loneliness. When one is oppressed by fear or guilt or anxiety or physical suffering or economic tension or family conflict, he is tempted to feel that no one else can possibly understand what he is facing. One is usually tempted to feel also that the efforts of other people to accept him are at the best well meaning but really unrelated, and at the worst are simply manipulative devices.

Loneliness at its root is a feeling of being cut off not only from other people in the sense that they neither know nor care, but also even from God. Every minister who has engaged in pastoral counseling has had people tell him, "I am beginning to doubt whether there is a God," when what they really mean is, (a) "I doubt whether whatever God there is cares for me," which in turn leads to, (b) "I doubt whether my life has any meaning or value." In other words, loneliness at its depth involves a kind of isolation in a solitary universe.

It is very difficult for a person who feels unlovable to accept the attempts of other people to be loving. It is very difficult for a person who feels morally tainted to let other people be understanding and accepting. It is very difficult for a person who feels terribly anxious to let other people, who are not apparently victims of the same fears, make contact with his heart. It is very difficult for one who is suffering excruciating physical pain to take seriously either that anyone else can appreciate what is going on, or that it makes any difference whether he does or not. The end result of all of this is that the sufferer feels helplessly and hopelessly alone.

In this sense loneliness also involves sin, and it cannot be dealt with unless there can be some communication of forgiveness. People not only feel cut off from God and man, they also feel that they somehow deserve this isolation and that this is the price they are having to pay for having sought self-fulfillment in some inappropriate manner. Much more important than the objective character of sin at this stage is the feeling on the part of the person seeking pastoral help that he is a sinner and therefore somehow disqualified from membership in the Israel of God. It doesn't help very much to tell him that he is accepted and wanted. Rather this has to be mediated to him through a life which may be focused in that of the pastor, but must certainly extend beyond him as an individual.

St. Paul wrote, *For God commendeth his love toward us, in that, while we were yet sinners, Christ died for us.* The heart of the New Testament proclamation is that God takes the initiative in breaking through the wall of loneliness behind which a person feels himself cut off from the Lord and from other men and women. God takes this action not because we have earned any such concern, but because we are the children of his love. He will not leave us in our solitary misery, and he uses human agents as his means of breaking through. Of course, this is beautiful theory on paper—but people have responded to the proclamation of the Gospel when they have heard it announced from the pulpit. In face-to-face situations the reality can become even more powerfully true.

Guilt and Moral Perfectionism

Loneliness in most instances is seriously compounded with guilt. The person who comes seeking help feels unworthy, even tainted, and he is sure that if any other person knew him for what he feels himself to be, that person would not have anything to do with him. The person who comes for help tends at the outset even to be unsure of the counselor's concern, should he discover the depth and blackness of the counselee's moral failure.

People who feel isolated from God and man tend to hate themselves. Since few people clearly admit even to themselves that they do this, there is usually an alternation, sometimes oscillating so rapidly that the counselor finds it difficult to relate to it, between bitter hostility toward other people—husband, wife, parents, children, employer, fellow-worker—and morbid self-recrimination. These feelings of self-hatred may sometimes be so deeply rooted that referral to a psychiatrist is called for; but even where the situation is not that serious, these feelings are found. Few situations in which there is not an element of self-hatred involving guilt will ever come to the attention of the pastoral counselor.

People come for help because of the load of guilt they are carrying, even when they are not clearly aware that this is a major cause of their cries for assistance. Since everybody has failed in many instances to fulfill the requirements both of his own code and of what society would expect, there is in every instance a sense in which the guilt is "real"—that is, involving the actual breach of some law. But guilt is never simply this, because questions immediately come up as to why the counselee need feel

the way he does. Is the standard which he feels himself
to have violated objectively valid? Is his behavior actually
susceptible of quite the interpretation he puts upon it,
granted that everybody is marked by some actual moral
failure? Indeed, is guilt the cause or the result of self-
hatred—in the sense that if one can keep telling himself
that he is morally tainted, then he is justified in down-
grading himself when perhaps there are other reasons for
his feelings of unworthiness?

Again, while the dealing with problems of guilt may
sometimes be beyond the capacity of a pastor and require
the skills of the psychiatrist, the fact remains that guilt is
a universal aspect of the problems leading to pastoral relationships. And guilt in the Twentieth Century is as often
as not compounded with a legacy of moralistic perfec-
tionism, derived from the Puritans, perhaps, and from the
Victorian social code; and this legacy guarantees moral
failure in advance. If the moral standards are too exalted
in their demands, every person is doomed in advance either
to failure or dishonesty or, in most instances, to a combina-
tion of the two.

There is no doubt that organized Christianity has contributed to the problems of guilt which oppress those who
seek aid in living with themselves and with others. The
tradition which presented the Sermon on the Mount as
a list of moral injunctions which the consecrated Christian was supposed to be quite capable of fulfilling, if he
took them with sufficient seriousness and worked hard
enough, has confused the New Testament with the Old,
and has turned our Lord's gift of spiritual freedom into
precisely the "Law" against which St. Paul strove in his
epistles. Men and women feel themselves doomed to be
either Pharisees or failures. Yet this false view of Christianity never really convinces them deep down in their

hearts, and they are not sure what they are. But the fact remains that the problem of guilt, regardless of how the details are derived and interpreted, is an inevitable part of the human experience in that people never fully live up to their own expectations of themselves and, at the same time, are continually tempted to ascribe a moral cause to circumstances which they find to be difficult.

If the pastor is to help a person work through his problem of guilt, that person has to be helped both to accept the fact that he is as he is, and to re-examine the meaning and purpose of his moral standards in a world where moral codes do have a function. Every pastor has had those who have come to see him say in one way or another, "The hardest thing for me to accept is your acceptance of me." Yet what the pastor is really trying to do is to dramatize dynamically, through life rather than words, that the God and Father of our Lord Jesus Christ cares, cares sufficiently for this lonely, guilt-laden son or daughter of Adam to meet him where he is now. God's love cannot be bought. It is freely given.

Every pastor has had occasions when people finally become free enough to express the hostility they feel toward others—a hostility which is gnawing at their hearts, and which they have tried ineffectively to suppress; and then these same people feel guilty for having said what they have, and once more even the question of the counselor's acceptance may arise. When people finally are facing up to the resentment they have toward their parents or children, or their husbands or wives, they have to deal once more with the "ideal" code which says that good, red-blooded, right-living men and women should not have such feelings. But they have them all right, and this is why they came to the pastor in the first place; and until they can be helped to feel that God meets them where they are, even with these feelings, the pastoral task is far from complete.

In the last analysis, guilt-laden people might be said to be crying for help because they have misread or have been more often mistaught the meaning of the second of the two great commandments which Jesus used to summarize the law and the prophets: *Thou shalt love thy neighbor as thyself.* Modern men and women do not love themselves enough. As the distinguished psychoanalyst, Erich Fromm, has pointed out, selfishness and self-love, rather than being identical, are opposites, and one cannot adequately deal with the problem of selfishness, destructive as it is to relationships with both God and man, until he is helped to love himself as one upon whose life the Most High God has set the mark of being lovable.

The Relationship to the Pastor

Because of the pressure of a person's need—whether it be physical, social, or emotional—he tends to turn every attempt to help him, which he is willing to accept even tentatively, into a relationship between himself and a specific person. The basis for this relationship may, where professional skills are involved, carry with it some conscious recognition of the connection between the professional skill and the personality of the helper. In the case of social workers, psychiatrists, and physicians this interpersonal pattern often results in at least a temporary feeling of dependency of the one who needs help upon the one who provides it. The experienced social worker, psychiatrist, and physician understand this and are able to work with it as one of the stages through which the person being helped passes on his way to recovery.

The psychotherapist quoted in the last chapter has also written:

The minister is often not clearly aware of what his parishioner is asking of him and may unconsciously share the false expectations which the other has. Many people come to the minister implicitly asking him to be first judge and then policeman, i.e., to enunciate and enforce the law, civil or moral. The unspoken, and sometimes even spoken, demand is that the minister read the riot act to an erring spouse or to objectionable neighbors. Paranoid people frequently make this kind of request. Others, especially women, come expecting the minister to be the ideal father or an ideal spouse.

Since the minister represents the authority of the Church, it is easy for people to confuse him with God and to expect him to act like him. The minister can find a great deal of relief by bringing such false expectations into his own clear awareness. Then he will cease to share them and will not suffer from the anxiety which sailing under false colors usually arouses, even when, or especially when, it is not entirely conscious. If a man is expected to be a policeman and he *is* a policeman, he does not have any psychological difficulty. He may be shot in line of duty, but he knows what he has to do. But if he allows someone to believe that he will act as a policeman, when he will not and cannot, he becomes uneasy. How much more is this the case when someone believes he will act as God! [1]

In the case of the Church, however, the pastor is not primarily the helper with skills, nor a friendly personality with whom one is acquainted. He is, above all, the representative of the Church in which both the sufferer and he belong and it is therefore very important, in order that

[1] Dr. Margaret J. Rioch, "Three Questions in Pastoral Counseling," *Journal of Pastoral Care, op. cit.*

the nature of pastoral care be not confused, that the context in which it is made available be made clear. Where the pastor allows dependency relationships to develop to any appreciable extent, not only his own function but even that of the Church is being compromised. For one thing, it is impossible for a person to be both dependent and equal in the same fellowship, so that to the extent he feels dependent he may no longer feel qualified to participate freely. To the extent that a transference develops to any real degree, to this extent also the nature of the sufferer's relationship to the Church is mixed up; because it is not the role of the pastor to serve any purpose whatever in relationship to his parishioner which cannot be integrated with the fellowship life they both share. Admittedly this concept of pastoral care is difficult to work out in practice. Yet it can be the living basis for a dynamic method of helping people.

The ministry of pastoral care is above all a ministry of patient loving, which attempts to communicate to people in trouble—even more by the dynamics of the contact than by the words used—that he or she is important and significant, not only to people who may have a kind of professional stake, but to the Lord God and the fellowship of his Holy People who represent him on earth.

The ministry of pastoral care begins with an attempt to help the person concerned rediscover his place in the fellowship of God's people. The pastor is first of all that member of the fellowship who is charged with the responsibility of making the concern of the Christian family something real and tangible to those who need to be reassured of its reality. Since one's feeling of participation in the life of the Christian Church tends, even under the best of circumstances, to be somewhat vague in meaning, special

55

help is needed in times of difficulty. It is the pastor's primary task, therefore, to make immediate and concrete what is all too often only theological.

Whatever special techniques and resources the pastor may have at his own command and whatever cooperative services seem desirable in helping the person in trouble to recover spiritual health, the distinctively Christian goal is the recovery of a sense of belonging—both as wanted, loved, accepted, and enabled to love and to accept—within the family of the People of God. It is our Christian objective, which the pastor mediates in the form of face-to-face encounter, that men and women be able to build their lives upon the conviction that *Neither death, nor life, nor angels, nor principalities, nor powers, nor things present, nor things to come, nor height, nor depth, nor any other creature, shall be able to separate us from the love of God, which is in Christ Jesus our Lord.*

CHAPTER V

CHRISTIAN FAITH
AND PASTORAL VISITING

The whole concept of the pastorate rests upon the conviction that the Almighty God cares for individual persons, for
families, for those who work wherever they work, and for
those seeking to find some way of making life meaningful regardless of the problems with which they contend.
As we have seen, the concern of God for his children is
primarily exercised through the instrumentality of the
Church, as the Holy People of God, inspired by the Holy
Spirit, seeking to make God's will effective in the world.
And if one aspect of what we believe to be God's will in the
Christian scheme of things is that human beings are important as persons, this aspect will become effective in
some form of a ministry of pastoral care.

The pastoral ministry may perhaps be divided into two
major areas of service, each of which can be subdivided
into special types of ministry aimed at meeting particular forms of human need. In any event, the two major
areas are: (1) outreach to people where they are, whether
or not they are asking for any particular help; and, (2)
availability to people who have special needs and who are
consciously desiring help even though they may be some-

57

what confused as to what they really need. There is a third important area, which theoretically is a subdivision of the second mentioned above, but practically resembles the first—the area of ministry to those who do need help but who, because of illness or age, have to be reached where they are rather than at the church.

In both major areas of the pastoral ministry, including the third whether under the first heading or under the second, the ordained clergy have the major responsibility for carrying on whatever is done, or of taking the initiative in seeing that a teamwork approach is made. In any event, the ordained minister will continue as the resource person helping others in various aspects of this ministry, and this is certainly preferable to thinking, feeling and acting as though the whole process depends solely upon him.

In the first area—outreach to people where they are —to a much greater extent than in the second, the ordained clergy are able to enlist the effective partnership of lay members of the congregation, provided that this is understood to be a partnership rather than to use auxiliary services or to give the laymen something to do. At the same time, the clergy cannot expect those who are being called on to regard the visit of a lay representative of the church as being the same thing as a call from the pastor himself. It may actually be more effective in terms of meeting people creatively and imaginatively, but there is a sense in which parishioners feel that they are entitled to the personal interest of their minister, and they need help at their end in understanding the doctrine of the Church, if they are not to regard the visit of lay callers as a kind of substitute service.

The laymen have a place in the pastoral ministry of the Church, and perhaps the most logical place for this is in the area of outreach—provided they understand themselves to be partners, and not salesmen, in the ministry of loving concern. There is no doubt that the Church needs to be working ever more experimentally toward defining the place of laymen in the pastoral ministry to the modern world—not as a substitute for the professional clergy, but rather as a distinctive ministry in its own right.

In the second area—availability to those with special needs—the full-time clergy will necessarily assume more direct responsibility because of their training and because of their control over their own time. Here partnership with lay people will take the form of cooperation with those who have special skills in the fields of medicine, psychiatry and social case work; and the responsibility for experimentation should be in the direction of finding more effective ways of interdisciplinary cooperation where there can be mutual respect and integrity.

This book is not a "How-to-do-it Book." Much has been written about techniques of the pastoral ministry in various areas. Rather this book is an attempt to place these various services rendered by the Church, under the general heading of the Ministry of Pastoral Care, in a perspective of Christian understanding so that what is done will make maximum sense. Then how this ministry is carried on in detail will be not so much a matter of techniques unrelated to theologically clear goals as it will be a matter of using the insights and skills which God has made available as clearly as possible in line with what we believe to be his will.

Parish Calling

Probably no aspect of the ministry of pastoral care is in greater need of this kind of clarification than the normal, routine service rendered by most parish clergymen in the course of what is known as parish visiting—calling at people's homes. It is generally understood that this is expected to be a major part of what a minister does, but neither clergymen nor lay people are very clear as to the theological significance of this activity. Consequently parish visiting becomes a source of very real anxiety for many clergymen because they are torn between a feeling that they ought to be going out calling and a mounting resistance against doing something which so often seems pointless. At the same time lay people, who have been conditioned to expect something in this line, tend to feel neglected when they do not find themselves getting it, yet are not too sure as to what they are missing.

This book, of its nature, cannot attempt to say when nor how parish calls should be made. Obviously circumstances will vary depending upon whether the members of a congregation know each other, the kind of other responsibilities the clergy have to assume, the nature of the neighborhood or city in which the particular parish serves, and all sorts of special conditions. What is done in the course of this visiting also depends upon a great many factors, including the realities of individual situations.

There is a purpose, however, in parish visiting regardless of the way detailed circumstances may influence what is actually done and how it is performed. Behind all pastoral visiting is this underlying assumption—God cares personally for Tom, Dick, and Harry, for Sally, Sue, and Jane. They are persons of importance to Almighty God, who has called them to find a place for themselves in his Holy People and who continues to reach out to them wherever they are and regardless of what otherwise concerns them. The call of the minister at a person's home, or at his place of business, is a practical reminder of that person's significance in God's scheme of things. The fact that many lay people never are really helped to discover that this is the purpose of the pastoral visit and that a great many clergymen seem to have forgotten it, if they ever knew it, in no way denies the underlying purpose. The clergy call because God cares and uses them as the spearhead of his concern. But the clergy will confuse this issue if they do all the calling themselves.

Pastoral visiting, aside from calling on the sick, the chronically ill and the shut-ins, which will be given special attention in the next section, may be divided into two major subdivisions: visiting those who are already identified in some manner with the congregation, and calling on those who are newcomers to the community and potential members of the parish. Because the former is so often the most irksome, we shall deal with it first.

Calling on Those Who Belong

Pastoral calling on those who are already identified in some manner with the congregation is a way the Church reflects its realistic awareness that individuals and families in actual life have more than one side to them. Because the same man may be a business executive, a parent, a taxpayer, a member of a political group, a member of a country club, a member of a civic organization, as well as a member of the Christian fellowship, it is very easy for these relationships to conflict with each other, thus leaving him at cross-purposes in the business of living. The Christian Church claims that kind of primary loyalty which in God's scheme of things brings order and harmony to all the other relationships people may have; but the congregation, in practice, usually becomes actually one more loyalty competing for time, energy, resources, and attention with other demands upon the same people. Therefore it is altogether too easy for men and women to find themselves confused.

It is not expected that the average parish call will, in and by itself, result in the reorientation of the person or family upon whom the call is made. Rather it is expected that the pastoral visit will provide a quasi-sacramental opportunity for a meeting to take place in the presence of God. No sacrament—not even Holy Communion—automatically re-orders the lives of those who receive. The purpose of any sacrament, however, is to reflect God's saving purpose in tangible form, thus providing a valuable and, in most situations, an indispensable occasion of God's purpose making contact with those whom he seeks to reach. Christ is the real priest in the celebration of any sacrament, whether at the altar or the doorbell, and the Church serves as his agent.

When a minister or a trained layman calls on a member of the congregation, he often has special reasons behind his visit. These can be terribly important; but it must be remembered that to the extent that they dominate the meeting between pastor and parishioner, this other underlying purpose is played down. It is important to encourage those who have been only nominally taking part in activities to take a more active interest. It is important to recruit lay leadership for the congregation's program. It is important to deal with the misunderstandings which arise whenever people work together for any length of time, in order that these may not disrupt more basic relationships. But it is also important—even more important—for men and women, for families, for those who are employed, to receive concrete reminders that God cares, when the representative of the congregation of God's Holy People in that concrete situation comes to call.

Perhaps one special note might be expressed here. Often a pastoral visit can result in a new sense of confidential relationship between the individual or family being called on and the pastor who makes the call. As this occurs, people may become free to raise problems requiring special attention. I do not believe that pastoral counseling, except under very special circumstances, can be done effectively in the setting of the ordinary pastoral visit. There are a number of practical reasons for this which will receive some attention in a later chapter. It is far better in most situations for the pastor to suggest that the person upon whom he is calling make an appointment and come to see him at his study, where the problem can be dealt with more quietly and unhurriedly than at home or in the office. Then both pastor and parishioner may indeed give prayerful thanks that the pastoral visit has become the opportunity for God's concern to become operative in more special ways.

It has been assumed in this discussion of the importance of pastoral visiting that local circumstances will indicate the relative emphasis placed upon this aspect of the ministry of pastoral care as against other areas of importance. It has also been assumed that the larger part of such pastoral visiting, in most situations, will take the form of calling at people's homes. There is, however, an important significance in making contact with people where they work, as occasion permits and in the light of such practical considerations as the interruption of work and taking time for which others are paying. Yet the fact remains that in most families there is at least one breadwinner, and that his or her occupation takes a large proportion of time and energy as well as of interest and imagination, especially if he is happily placed; while there will be frustrations growing from his job, if he is not happily situated. If God cares about people as persons, he is certainly concerned with the way they think of themselves in the course of working. While the problem of

Christian vocation in the Twentieth Century can no more be solved through pastoral visiting at places of business than the problem of the family can be solved by calls at homes, still there is the need for objectively expressing God's concern for his children in the basic settings in which they live. The congregation exists in order to care, and the clergymen serve to focus that concern.

In spite of all the useful and important things which can be dealt with when a clergyman calls on an individual or a family belonging to the congregation, the basic fact remains: the pastoral visit has meaning in its own right. We who are in the professional ministry call because God cares; and it is important for us to give sufficient opportunity for this type of personal concern in our own schedules to feel the sacramental significance of pastoral visiting and to know the truth in our own hearts. Indeed, without some real place for that kind of pastoral visiting which has no other purpose than to express God's concern for persons as persons, it is doubtful whether the other and more specialized aspects of the ministry of pastoral care will be as meaningful as they could be.

Calling on New People

It is usually much easier to find a rationale for calling on prospective contacts than it is for what is often called "routine parish calling." New faces are seen at church services, and names and addresses may be secured at the church door. New children are brought to the church school, and it is obvious that they have families from which they come. Members of the congregation report that new neighbors appear to be interested in what the church is doing. In any one of a number of ways, from the Welcome Wagon to letters from mutual friends, word is received that people with the same denominational background have come into the community. It seems only natural to call to make them welcome and, incidentally, to encourage their affiliation with this particular congregation.

Reaching out to newcomers and to prospective new members is certainly one of the important tasks in which the professional clergyman may expect concerned lay members of the congregation to share the load. Many techniques—sector plans, block captains, calling committees, and the like—have been developed to make this lay responsibility effective. In many parishes tremendous energy goes into the task of recruiting new individuals and families for membership.

Precisely because this business of calling on newcomers seems such a natural and logical thing to do, there is very real danger that its underlying purpose will be overlooked. The outreach in God's scheme of things is a fundamental aspect of the ministry of pastoral care rather than the kind of "rushing" competition that marks college fraternities. The congregation, as local representative of God's Holy People, is meant to be concerned with new opportunities for service rather than with making sales.

In other words, behind the outreach to newcomers is a basic question; and until it is answered honestly and searchingly by those who make the calls, one can hardly expect those who are called upon to appreciate the deeper meaning of what is going on. The question is this: *What does church membership consist of in God's scheme of things?* In other words, why should people identify themselves with the Christian movement in general, to say nothing of this local congregation in particular?

This author has tried a number of experiments using the device known as role-playing, informal spontaneous dramatizations in which people play their assigned parts by ear as they think these would be handled in daily life.

With both clergy groups and lay groups he has used the situation of a minister's call on a new family in the community. Rarely, if ever, has the concept of the Church as God's Holy People, in which men and women find their true heritage, come into the conversation even by suggestion. In very few role-plays, if any, has there been any mention of the congregation as the local representative fellowship which makes God's saving love known and felt. Usually the discussion has been on the convenient arrangements for the church school, the interesting groups which meet in connection with parish life, the music, and the obligation—expressed but not explained—of people to take part in parish life.

Yet calling on new people can be a tremendously important part of the ministry of pastoral care. We call because God is concerned, and he uses men and women as the instrumentalities through whom he expresses his loving care. We call in order to be of the greatest possible service—which means not so much presenting a catalogue of available resources like a brush salesman at the door of a prospective customer—we call because we care for those upon whom we call, care for them as persons, as children of God. Therefore we call to listen.

If the ministry of pastoral care is the underlying presupposition of whatever process a parish church may develop for reaching newcomers, one thing is certain: there will be an effective spiritual resistance to the natural human tendency to go after "scalps," to build up a sales record. Rather, the conscious purpose of the caller will be to help those whom he visits to discover that they are important as persons, because God loves them and sent his Son to die for them. In most situations this message can only be communicated by indirect suggestion and not stated in so many words; we live in an age where pious technicalities make people suspicious and uneasy. We also live in a salesman's era, and it is natural for anyone approached by another to ask, "What is his angle?" Yet people can sense that others really care, without some ulterior motive, provided the pastoral caller is patient, and responsive, and warm.

The process of calling on newcomers can be a most important instrument for making the more specialized aspects of the ministry of pastoral care seem genuine.

CHAPTER VI

CHRISTIAN FAITH
AND PASTORAL COUNSELING

While the pastoral ministry of calling on those who are already identified with the congregation, even on those who are prospective church members, is of its nature diffuse and extensive, that aspect of pastoral care which takes the form of conferences in the minister's study is the reverse. It is very particular and intensive. In the former type of ministry the pastoral visit expresses symbolically and quasi-sacramentally the fact that God cares for people as persons. In the latter they come with at least some dim feeling, perhaps described in non-religious terms or as only a wistful hope, that their problems will be taken seriously by someone who represents God's love.

A great deal has been written on pastoral counseling from the standpoint of attempting to synthesize Christian ideas with the insights of psychiatry. It is not necessary to try to do this again in this chapter, except to underline the importance for the professional ministry in this mid-period of the Twentieth Century to become as knowledgeable as possible in the fields of psychiatry, medicine and social case work, particularly where these seem to share common ground with religion. *This book assumes the necessity of clinical training as part of the preparation for the ministry,* because there is no substitute to being confronted, under supervision, with people who are victims of emotional or social breakdown. This book further assumes the necessity for clergymen not only to have had the opportunity to observe human abnormality—as exaggerated demonstrations of normal behavior traits such as would be found in hospitals, prisons and mental institutions—it also assumes the tremendous value of giving ministers some insight into the way their own personalities function, insights gained from psychotherapy, and interpersonal groups under trained leaders.

In the chapter, "Pastoral Care and the Self-Understanding of the Minister," we discussed the way the clergyman sees his own professional role in distinction from, yet in cooperation with, other specialized disciplines—the physician, the psychiatrist, and the social caseworker. In the chapter, "Why Do People Turn to The Church?" there was a treatment of some of the hopes and expectations in the minds of those who come to the pastor's study. Our concern here is with the basic significance of what happens when they meet.

When the minister, in his role as pastor, sits down for a face-to-face conference with an individual or a family in difficulty, he is responsible both to God and to the congregation whose concern he focuses. Because he is human himself, his own feelings will play some part, and his effectiveness is not so much a result of eliminating his feelings as it is of understanding them and being able to live with them. The people who come for help are also human, and they will probably hide, even from full conscious recognition in themselves, the deeper problems which disturb them; and patient, concerned listening is needed to discover what the shooting is all about, and whether this situation is one calling for referral to specialized services or one which the pastor ought to handle himself. Yet this business of self-understanding and patience is not simply a matter of technical training, important as training is. It is an evidence of God's love, expressed through imperfect instruments, to be sure, yet still expressed.

On the one hand, the solemn obligation to serve the Most High God in the pastoral conference is so important that every possible skill should be made available to serve; pious good intentions and sympathetic feelings are not a substitute for insight and appreciation, for what they are, of "ills that flesh is heir to." On the other hand, the number of people asking for help—rather, groping for some kind of guidance—in living with themselves is so great that the technical, psychiatric, and social service resources in the community cannot hope to do more than handle the more serious problems.

The ministry of pastoral care, therefore, in the form of the counseling interview in the pastor's study is a necessity calling for both the best equipment the minister can bring to the task, and also for his making available a reasonable amount of time for seeing men and women who often have no other place to turn. When it is remembered that despite all attempts at educating people to feel the contrary, there is still a kind of stigma attached to the need for psychiatry and social case work; and furthermore, there is usually such a high financial cost involved in the former, that the need for this aspect of the ministry is even more obvious.

When all this has been said, however, the fact remains that the counseling interview is first of all an act in which the Church, through its professional clergyman, seeks to make God's concern known and felt by those in need. The clergyman is never the technical specialist operating in his own right, regardless of the training he may have had—indeed ought to have had. He is always the agent of God's love, deriving his authority from God's Holy People. He is accepting of people's self-disclosures involving all the various deviations from, and aberrations of the social code, not merely because he has a disciplined mind and is therefore not too easily shocked, but because God cares for his children because they *are* his children. He expresses God's forgiveness, whether in the ritual form of pronouncing absolution in the Sacrament of Penance, or in some more informal way—not because he is broadminded personally, but because God chooses to use him as an instrument of reconciliation in the cause of helping lonely, disturbed people find themselves a place in God's family.

All this is theory. It can only become living and effective in actual situations where pastors and people meet. People only find the love of God translated into a living force for their lives when they encounter it in real situations. And the pastor, from the nature of his duties, may be the most effective agent for making this dream come true.

Making Time Available

If the pastor really intends to serve effectively as an agent through whom God's loving concern can be expressed in concrete situations, he needs to let people know that he is available for conferences. This is more than a matter of posting office hours on the study door and announcing them in the Sunday leaflet. It is communicated by people to each other through experience as they discover that the minister will take time to see them unhurriedly and without interruptions.

A good deal might be said about the way time is planned, but this writer believes that pastoral counseling should, except in emergency situations, be by appointment made in advance on the initiative of the person who desires to talk over his problems. The suggestion might be made that the pastor would be glad to see him in the study, if the prospective counselee wishes to make an appointment (if possible through a secretary). Furthermore, since most counseling relationships will involve a series of interviews, it is better for the pastor to terminate the initial conference at a specified time. In later interviews the counselee can make his own plans with this time schedule in mind. The conference will not be cut primarily to save the minister's time for other activities, but rather as an indication of a responsible use of time on the part of both the counselor and the counselee—and time is one of God's gifts to be used in serving his purpose. The interview might well be ended after forty-five minutes or an hour, except in emergency situations; but under normal conditions other people trying to see the minister, or to reach him on the telephone, have a right to expect to know when they may be able to do so.

Word will get around if the pastor makes time available to those who wish to consult him, and particularly if he arranges affairs so that they are uninterrupted during the interview. There is nothing that can be more effective in communicating to a person that he has significance in his own right, and that his worries and anxieties are taken seriously, than an uninterrupted consultation period, when neither the telephone nor the demands of other people are allowed to interfere. If part of the purpose of pastoral counseling is to help men and women to know that God cares for them as persons and is concerned with the details of their lives—with nothing too unimportant to warrant attention and nothing so evil that it cannot have a hearing —then the tone of appointment setting and keeping speaks more convincingly than words.

A word needs to be said at this point about the importance of selectivity in planning the use of time available for counseling. Certainly not all problems are of equal importance, and certainly not every counseling relationship requires the same week-by-week schedule of conferences over an extended period. There are some unfortunate souls whose minds have become stuck like a needle on a cracked record, and harm rather than good may result from encouraging them to keep on repeating themselves. There are other people who are trying to deal with their very real difficulties by telling the same story first to this person and then to someone else; such a pattern can be destructive in the long run. Certainly every person, as a child of God, is entitled to be taken seriously in God's name in an uninterrupted counseling interview; but what happens afterwards depends on the needs of the situation as the minister best understands it.

Effective counseling normally involves a regular pattern of conferences, usually at the same hour on the same day every week for a period of weeks or months. In most situations the minister will have to suggest to the counselee the desirability of such an arrangement, since the lay person will have had little experience which would lead him to ask for this kind of service. Even though the initiative in many cases has to be taken by the minister, it will serve little purpose unless the counselee freely wishes to take part. In every situation it is important that the counselee, himself, bear some responsibility both for establishing the schedule and for determining how long and how regularly it shall run, rather than merely to acquiesce in the prescription of a so-called "expert." At the same time, however, the minister, as well as the counselee, assumes responsibility for proposing the termination of the series when he feels no further usefulness is being served.

In situations where it does not seem advisable to continue a repetitive process, it is not only a question of avoiding something difficult, but perhaps of suggesting that continually telling the same story will not get anywhere. This does not deny God's basic concern, but rather suggests that perhaps there is a need to dig more deeply with whatever counselor this person chooses. If there is no response on this level, appointments may just have to be postponed. In the case of the person who goes first to one advisor and then to another, perhaps the minister is most advantageously situated to suggest that this person make a choice and stick to it bearing in mind that such a shifting from one advisor to another may often be a way of refusing to face problems. God can use persons other than the minister to evince his concern for people, and it is a question of helping the person to realize that he will get more help by a consistent relationship than by changing at will.

There Are Limits to What Can Be Done

The basic principle is that, within the limits of human possibility, everybody who asks is entitled to be heard; but there will be many situations in which the first interview will be the only one. There will be situations brought to the minister's attention—because he is available and because there is a feeling that he can be trusted—which ought to be handled instead by a psychiatrist or social agency. More will be accomplished by making this suggestion within the context of trust, interpreting what the services of the psychiatrist and social worker are, and even pointing out how to make appointments with particular doctors or workers. Again this does not deny God's concern, but rather makes his care that much more effective in a world where he has so designed individual human nature and society that people are meant to complement each other rather than to try all alone to carry every load that comes along.

Patience is often required in helping a counselee accept the need for more specialized service, often several interviews are necessary. Sometimes it has to be left on the basis of "or else," because the minister has reached the end of his resources and no useful purpose will be served for God or anybody by pretending the contrary. At the same time, those who are referred to people with more specialized skills and training need to be assured that this is a transfer for service only, rather than a dismissal from the Church's responsibility, or from God's care.

It is only natural that the pastor will want to see his counseling turn out "successfully," in the sense that the problems which brought the counselee to his study become more clearly understood and the pressures disappear, so that the person himself is able to meet life more comfortably. Because this is true, ministers will tend to make time more easily available to those persons with whom a conference series leads to results than to those with whom it drags on and on without appearing to get anywhere. Within certain cautious limits there is justification in using limited time where it will be most productive, provided this is not an excuse for preferring pleasant relationships to difficult ones or interesting encounters to dull meetings. It is one of God's mercies that we are not really able to measure the success of interpersonal work while it is in process, and every experienced counselor learns that those who no longer need his help tend to drift away because they feel able to handle their own problems by themselves. More often than not he learns this only after noticing that it has been some time since he last had conferences with them, while those with whom he has not accomplished very much continue to return. God does not let clergymen measure pastoral success by statistics, but every now and then a pastor will be told by someone with whom he worked years previously that their meetings provided a turning point in life.

Finally, there are situations where the minister in the very name of God's concern must refuse someone after the initial conference, or even a series of conferences, because that person does not really desire to face his situation. Those who work with alcoholics know that unless the person concerned admits he has a problem and knows himself seriously to need help, endless time can be spent with nothing resulting. The same thing is true in other situations. It is not a denial of God's concern for a minister, after doing the best he can to develop a constructive relationship with a person needing help and even after making other resources available, to refuse further conferences until there is some evidence of a response. Such a decision is not made easily or happily, but it is part of pastoral responsibility.

What Is the Counselor Doing?

In every relationship with people who come to his study for counsel, the pastor is aware of his own limitations both as a person and as a professional advisor. He is not God. He is not even God's agent in any sense which implies that he has a pipeline of understanding not available to any reasonably intelligent, serious, and consecrated person, clerical or lay. He serves to focus the concern of the fellowship of God's Holy People, and this means that he takes to heart the difficulties of those who come to see him, because the people behind the problems are important in the sight of God.

Any pastor in the counseling role will experience many situations in which he hears people telling him about problems in their lives which he knows all too well to exist in his own personal affairs. If the pastor has any basic honesty, can he hear a man express doubt as to the purpose of his life, his vocation, his sense of objective, without the pastor himself recalling inwardly that he also is not always too sure where he is going? Can a married minister listen to people tell of their confusion in family life without some awareness that there are areas of confusion, too, in his family relationships? The point can be illustrated in every area of human anxiety and guilt. The pastor does not seek to work with those who come to him as if he himself were a person who did not have these kinds of problems, or had them all solved, but rather as a fellow child of God whom the Most High, in his inscrutable wisdom, still chooses to use as his agent for communicating saving acceptance, forgiveness, and love.

In other words, the pastor as a human being has his own difficulties in accepting himself for who he is. Like any other son of Adam, he is never as ready to trust God's forgiving love for himself as he is to recognize the intellectual truth in trying to help someone else. He has his own needs for self-justification, which he may know intellectually to be unnecessary; yet in his heart, so to speak, he feels the question. But perhaps it is really as the pastor lives with his own unsolved problems in the presence of God that he is that much more useful as the servant of the Holy People of God in sharing a faith that has power. Whether or not he tells any particular counselee that he is also a "stranger and pilgrim" along the same road depends upon how he feels that person's need will be best helped, but there is no minister worth his salt who has not gained insight into his own life as he has tried to be of service to others who were walking along the same lonely way.

As the counselor himself is not a person who has all problems solved and has no further doubts to perplex him, reaching down a helping hand to those below him on the climb to certainty, what is he doing? Perhaps this question ought first to be answered in the negative. He is not trying to let people down easily in the sense of trying to assuage life's pain without making some serious attempt to deal with the causes of the pain. It goes without saying that people can be given a temporary release through "spiritual tranquilizers" which have much the same effect as the chemical ones; and while there is obviously a place for both kinds of short-cutting, no tranquilizer is itself a therapy. A man can develop a popular reputation by blandly listening to other people's difficulties, giving out easy pat-on-the-back answers which have the temporary effect of making people feel that life is again worth living and that guilt has been unloaded. Yet it is not so much the task of the pastor as counselor to make life pleasant for people as it is for him to help them find a place in God's scheme of things where they can accept themselves, because they know themselves to be accepted without any deception. His goal is that they dare to make their own these lines: *Almighty God, unto whom all hearts are open, all desires known, and from whom no secrets are hid; Cleanse the thoughts of our hearts by the inspiration of thy Holy Spirit . . .*

If the pastor, as counselor, is not letting people down easily through the use of "spiritual Milltown," neither is he acting as an inscrutable oracle, the embodiment of wisdom beyond normal, mortal ken. Again, a man can acquire a reputation for profundity in dealing with human problems by playing the role of "the Great Stone Face." Stephen Leacock once said that the secret of a British education is "being smoked at by an educated man," and there are those who apply the same technique in dealing with human distress. There is certainly a place for completely non-directive counseling in psychiatry, and even the minister as counselor hesitates in playing any kind of directive role. Yet there is a place in his relationship with those who come for help where he can evince warm interest in them as persons. God's acceptance involves more than the pastor not being shocked by stories of human deviation. It involves also some indication that God cares for these people as themselves and has a place for them in the fellowship of his children.

The Sacrament of Penance

This chapter needs a note on the Sacrament of Penance—the confession by the individual penitent in the presence of a clergyman, who pronounces absolution in the name of God. The process is known, of course, as auricular confession and is a resource in the Episcopal and Lutheran Churches as well as in the Church of Rome, and to a certain extent has a place in other communions. While the rite may be used very infrequently, if at all, in many churches, and while its significance is not very well understood even by the most church-conscious lay people, it can be very valuable in the pastoral ministry to guilt and anxiety when used with discretion and in the context of a wider counseling ministry.

It goes without saying that anything told the pastor in a counseling interview in his study is just as much "under the seal of the confessional" as if it were told at the altar rail or in a confessional box. It is a privileged communication which can never be divulged, even under threat of contempt of court, without the uncoerced consent of the confessor. If people are really going to deal honestly and deeply with what is on their minds, they need to be able to trust the confidence of the pastor to whom they speak —and the ritual setting of the conversation is quite beside the point.

Again, it goes without question that an ultimate, though not immediate, purpose of the counseling relationship is to enable the person who comes to accept God's forgiveness to live with himself and with his past experience, without being broken by his knowledge and interpretation of his own failures. The purpose of the ritual pronouncement is to affirm this forgiveness dramatically and dynamically. It does not create it, but rather nails down—where it is used—a relationship to God and other people which has already been realized in principle.

Any use of auricular confession, within the understanding of this approach to Christian faith and pastoral care, will be essentially non-moralistic. Certainly questions of guilt involve moral considerations, but these are not arbitrary and external in their rigidity, rather they are guideposts along life's way as man's moral sensitivity and social experience have developed them.

The approach described here is the opposite from that underlying Roman Catholic theory, if not always Roman Catholic practice, and the taking over of such theory and practice by clergymen in non-Roman churches. In the Roman system, human behavior is classified in the greatest detail, and deviations from the prescribed norm are listed as either venial (routine) or mortal (very serious) on the basis of *a priori* judgments rather than the needs of individual personalities. Our concern, however, is with the confusion and guilt that individual men and women experience. The pastoral counselor obviously cannot act as if any kind of behavior were all right regardless of norms or standards; nevertheless, his major concern is with helping a person find his identity within the fellowship of the Church so that his behavior problems can be seen in a different light. The emphasis is on God's prior acceptance and forgiveness waiting to be received, rather than on human guilt.

The Sacrament of Penance has a valid place among the resources which the Church may use in helping troubled people, once it is understood that its purpose is to make overt an experience of honest awareness in the presence of God, and the acceptance of the fact that God loves even unlovely people. Any use of penance will certainly be determined by a mutually understood desire between the pastor and the person making the confession for some satisfactorily symbolic way of completing the act of re-stored fellowship—with one's self, with one's neighbor, and with one's God—rather than of earning pardon and peace.

The role of the clergyman as confessor—as the one who listens to the admission of moral failure—can be very helpful because often people find themselves freer to talk in this somewhat stylized relationship than in a face-to-face setting. On the other hand, there are very real problems. The structure of auricular confession places the accent on the professional status of the confessor rather than upon him as an individual person; and in the Roman Church (as well as to some extent in the Episcopal Church) those who avail themselves of the Sacrament of Penance may prefer to go to some parish where they are completely unknown so that personality factors may be eliminated entirely. This would seem to indicate that where people are sufficiently familiar with the Sacrament of Penance to want to use it, their concern tends to be with God's forgiveness as mediated through the Church's structure; and the element of trust or confidence in an individual is so secondary to the respect for his official function as to make it almost inconsequential. When people gain confidence primarily from the institutional structure of the Church, there is no doubt that they often receive a sense of inward peace and release; but there may be doubt as to whether their underlying needs have been adequately handled.

While the structure of auricular confession and the Sacrament of Penance may make it possible for some people more freely to admit what is on their minds, by the same token it makes it very difficult to get behind what the penitent confesses to the underlying problem. If all that were called for were a deeper probing along the lines of traditional moral theology, particularly as this has been developed by the Jesuits, relating the penitent's problem to the catalogues of venial and mortal sins, a skilled confessor could doubtless accomplish much. In most instances, however, this is not the problem despite what many advocates of auricular confession claim. What is called for is a free discussion of the fears, hostilities, and conflicts which underlie the behavior pattern, and this can be done much more adequately in the informal setting of counseling than it can in the formalized relationship of the confessional. In many cases, when the penitent is asking for absolution, he is seeking to avoid facing the root problems in his life; and instead of an easy ritual compliance with his request, referral to a psychiatrist may be indicated.

There is another angle which ought to be mentioned in this general context. The confessional process in many instances tends to focus the penitent's attention on superficial behavior problems, and indeed to encourage the penitent to think that these have an importance which, as a matter of fact, they do not have. Whereas in creative counseling relationships the sequence is eventually broken and the counselee sent out on his own to deal with life with the new strength and insight he has acquired—the latchstring out in case he needs to come back—in the confessional the opposite is true. There is no end to this pattern, and instead of encouraging the penitent to grow up so as to handle his own affairs, he is rather encouraged to keep returning even if the only things he has to talk about are piddling.

In spite of the limitations and dangers in too formal a use of the Sacrament of Penance, nevertheless it can often become the way by which the pastor concludes a series of counseling interviews dealing with guilt in its various ramifications. When the situation seems to have been explored as thoroughly as necessary, and when the meaning of the pastoral relationship as evincing God's acceptance and concern seems to be reasonably well appreciated, then it is sometimes helpful to tie the strings together with the sacramental act. From the standpoint of this writer, however, the counseling relationship in the study can be as essentially sacramental as that performed more formally. Indeed, if the setting in the study is not felt to be in the presence of God's love, that in the church tends to become externally mechanical.

Without presuming to generalize on when and how this ancient resource of communicating God's forgiving love should be used, it is probably wisest to make it available only after a sufficiently complete counseling relationship. Even the historic rites of the Church can be used as spiritual tranquilizers, and this the pastor seeks to avoid at all costs. Only when he and the counselee both realize that they have gone beneath the surface feelings of guilt and confusion to the more important level of the orientation of a life, can they dramatize this feeling in the confidence that this is reality.

CHAPTER VII

CHRISTIAN FAITH
AND THE
MINISTRY TO THE SICK

Probably the most obvious area of pastoral concern in which the Church reaches out through its clergy is the ministry to the sick. Ministers who find it difficult to do the kind of pastoral visiting envisioned in Chapter V accept calling on the sick as a natural responsibility. Clergymen who are uncertain as to what can be accomplished in a counseling interview in the study find it no strain to go to the hospital room. Regardless of how effectively this ministry may be performed, it is taken for granted that the sick have a claim upon the Church's attention and that the clergy must make adequate provision for this service in planning their work.

When recognition has been given to the fact that the Christian tradition in the modern day assumes that the pastoral care of the sick is important, it is sometimes forgotten that there are aspects to this ministry which do not receive the same attention—either because of their difficulty or because the long-time, little changing problem tends to lose urgency in its appeal for help. Those who are in hospitals for operations and emergency illnesses and those who have had serious accidents usually receive the Church's attention as a matter of course; but those who are infirm because of age or chronic ailments dragging on for months and years, and those in mental institutions as a rule do not receive the same concern. While the excuse is often given that these situations can wait for a day or so, as they are going to continue in much the same way for an indefinite period, *mañana* is sometimes an indefinite postponement and the alibi for failing to try to deal with a difficult problem.

The ministry to the sick, regardless of the type of physical or mental difficulty afflicting people, involves visiting the ill people where they are rather than expecting them to come to the minister. In this sense, this note of pastoral care resembles other aspects of pastoral visiting. On the other hand, those who are seriously ill, chronically sick, or emotionally disturbed may have difficulties in their relationships to God and man requiring the special kind of sensitivity of the counseling interview. The basic principle of pastoral concern, however, is still the same: those who are being cared for are children of God, of importance as persons to the Most High, and therefore a responsibility for his agency, the Holy People, and a charge upon the conscious concern of those who focus the work of the Church.

The ministry to the sick can, of course, be subdivided into the areas mentioned and to even more minute classifications, and much has been written about it from a technical standpoint. This discussion, therefore, will not attempt to deal so much with the special understandings which are helpful and often necessary in the hospital, the nursing home, the mental institution, and in the sickroom at home as well, but rather will seek to suggest how this aspect of pastoral care can be that much more significant as it manifests the nature of the Church.

The Social Setting of Illness

Just as there needs to be a background of training and understanding to the counseling aspects of the pastoral ministry, so there needs to be guidance in understanding how most effectively to perform this ministry to the sick. Training in this area is increasingly becoming part of the regular seminary program of preparing candidates for the ministry, and graduate courses and special summer training programs have become available in many metropolitan areas. Along with the need for special insights in what is to be expected in ministering to the ill, and how best to respond to their needs, is also a need for some concern for the social aspects of the problem. On the whole, those who are treated for emergency illness or undergo operations in standard hospitals receive excellent physical care, and some of the better private institutions for the emotionally disturbed have excellent programs. The same cannot be said for the care of the chronically ill, particularly of the aged. By and large, nursing homes meet only minimum standards for crowding and convenience and warm, friendly interest—though there are notable exceptions. While some state hospitals have high standards and effective programs, there is a general problem of too great a load upon the personnel for the best interests of the patients, and in many such hospitals care is more custodial than therapeutic.

It is important for the pastor to be aware of this lack of resources for the adequate care of some types of illness, not just because he is supposed to be a socially concerned citizen, but even more because the problems resulting from ineffective treatment bear upon both the patients themselves and upon those who love them and who are responsible for them. When men and women find themselves placed on some kind of social shelf because the community either does not know what to do with them or has not faced the responsibility for adequate care, it is very hard for these people to maintain for very long any convictions as to their own value as persons. When those who are related to patients in such a plight have explored every possible area for resources which they can afford, and which will be helpful, and then reach the end of their ropes, they, too, need pastoral help. Both the patients and the members of their families are meant to understand themselves as the children of a God who cares, and this is not too easy. One group feels itself to be on the social scrap heap, and the other to be inextricably involved in guilt for the apparent neglect of those for whom they are responsible, with nothing that can be done to change the situation.

In other words, the social setting of the problem of illness is necessarily of concern to the pastor who seeks to communicate God's concern to people in trouble. Along with recognizing those areas of human physical and mental distress where community resources are inadequate, he needs also to be conscious of the effect of the high cost of illness, which is not only an economic problem but a spiritual one, raising issues of resentment and guilt, feelings that neither God nor mankind really cares, and that people are caught in a hopeless trap. Certainly the pastor cannot expect to be able to solve these monetary problems any more than he can supply adequate nursing homes for the elderly or adequate staffs for state hospitals. But he can live shoulder-to-shoulder as the brother-in-God with those who have to face these problems with no viable alternatives. The concerned minister will recognize that to the extent these insoluble difficulties press in upon both the patients and upon their families, it will be that much more difficult for them to accept the proclamation of God's love as being more than words. Therefore, he seeks to love through sharing the pain, even when he cannot see any final remedy.

The Pastor's Own Role

The ministry to the sick requires a special effort to make clear the pastor's role as the focus of the love of God's Holy People refusing to let go of persons who are physically prevented from taking part in the congregation's life and also walled in on themselves by their own suffering. Therefore, the minister's call is functionally different from the visit of a kind, well-meaning and understanding friend, even one who is knowledgeable about the problems of the sickroom.

The pastoral care of the sick is not limited to the ordained clergy in principle, although in practice here is an area where it is often much more effective for the minister, himself, to represent the concern of the Holy Fellowship. In the ministry to those in general hospitals, in nursing homes, and also to those convalescing in their own residences, however, there is very real room for trained and sensitive lay people to play a most valuable part through their visits in reminding the invalids that they are important and cared for. In the case of patients in mental hospitals, on the other hand, such lay partnership in the ministry to the sick is not usually possible or desirable, since the nature of the situation demands more controls over visitors and more understanding on the part of those who call.

Whoever calls in the name of the Church is never merely an individual, but always is the earnest of the Christian fellowship, and whatever is done derives its basic meaning from this fact. Whether lay visitors or the ordained clergy are involved, the same principle holds true. While, in a very real sense, this insight applies equally to every area in which the pastoral responsibility is shared, it has a peculiar pertinence here in that the special training and sensitivity required of those who call on the ill should be understood not only from the technical standpoint but also from the theological. Those who assume such a ministry at the same time accept a stewardship of the mysteries of God.

In the ministry to the sick, the responsibility of the congregation as a whole and of lay visitors who share in discharging this task is underlined by what must be expected of the ordained minister. Certainly it is desirable that he be conversant with the special needs of sick people and how best they can be helped. It is very useful that he have some training in how to relate himself to those involved more directly with the therapy. It is essential that he himself be sensitive to the feelings and needs of the people upon whom he is calling. Yet all of these are secondary to the fact that he ceases to be a pastor if he calls as an individual. The pastor who is calling upon the sick is in a very real sense surrogate for the entire fellowship which he serves. It is inexpedient and impractical that several hundred people troop simultaneously through the sickroom and together offer corporate prayer or sacramental ministrations. The minister's call does this for all and it goes without saying, therefore, that behind the act of calling pastorally upon the ill should be the ministry of prayer in the congregational life when that which is performed symbolically by the sick call becomes articulate in some real sense in the experience of other lay people.

Another important aspect of the theological meaning of the ministry to the sick becomes apparent when we realize that such pastoral care includes, where possible, not only the patient but his family, and his closest friends where this is possible. In many cases of illness, the family suffer either from anxiety as to the outcome or from guilt arising from the annoyances they feel at being put out by having to readjust their plans in the light of the sickness. In many instances a family or close friends need more direct pastoral attention than the patient. This may be complicated by the fact that these persons may not actually belong in the same parish as the patient. Nevertheless, the Christian fellowship has a ministry to those who are tied to its members, and the pastor's acts are representative of this.

The Ministry to the Chronically Ill

One of the most difficult parts of the whole ministry of pastoral care is to the chronically ill, or shut-ins. These people are prevented by physical breakdown from participating in any form of community life, and the course of their illness drags on for months, if not for years. The ministry to the aging is similar to the extent that it refers to those whose physical breakdown is the result of gradual degeneration through advancing years.

The reason that the ministry to the shut-ins is so difficult is that those who undertake it cannot help but be aware that the persons to whom they minister will never return to full and active life within the fellowship of the Holy People of God. Therefore the task of the Church becomes one of continually reaching out to those whose response can never be very complete and who offer no promise of ever being able to make a fuller response at a later date. Since the chronically ill or shut-ins remain pretty much the same day by day, week by week, year by year, it is also rather easy to forget one's pastoral responsibility for them since a call one time will serve about the same purpose as a call another time; whereas in dealing with the physically ill in hospitals the clergyman has a feeling that he is helping to deal with an emergency. When it comes to dealing with the chronically ill, he does not have this feeling, and sometimes is disturbed as to what actually he is accomplishing. While it is true that many of the people in this category appreciate attention, the question cannot help but be considered whether their need for some "fresh air" in the otherwise protracted, dull routine of a long period of incapacity precludes any real appreciation of the context in which the pastoral visit is supposed to be made.

It is important that clergymen have areas of responsibility where they cannot see any direct result accruing from their work, lest they forget that their primary function is to focus the concern of God's Holy People for persons who are born to be children of God, rather than to serve as experts in their own individual right. If the ministry to the chronically ill and the shut-ins accomplished no other purpose, it would be helpful in this regard. But just because results cannot be measured, and in spite of the fact that expressions of appreciation from those called on seem sometimes to be beside the point, it does not mean that nothing creative happens. The Church's concern is not dependent upon the ability of those who are loved to articulate what they take their experience to mean, any more than the love of mothers is dependent upon the way babies respond. The important fact is that God cares and refuses to let go, even when society has exhausted what it knows how to do or the responsibilities it is ready to assume. The pastor in his calls upon the chronically ill and the shut-ins serves to make this truth real.

The Ministry to Mental Institutions

While a good deal has been written about the ministry to the emotionally disturbed, including those in mental institutions, something needs to be said here in the context of this book. This type of pastoral care will differ from other forms of ministry to the sick in its need for the minister to fit what he is trying to do into what the hospital staff has planned. It cannot be the clergyman's job to call the signals, but in most cases he will find at least some readiness to accept him as a resource—even by psychiatrists who are themselves quite vague as to the operations of organized religion—provided he is willing to be open to suggestion.

The ministry to those in mental institutions is complicated by the fact that very often their illusions involve religious symbols. The patients may frequently appear to be asking speculative theological and philosophical questions when as a matter of fact their problems have quite a different focus. In those mental hospitals where there is adequate provision for a chaplaincy service, and the clergymen involved have had special training and also sit in on staff conferences, the visiting pastor may be able to find help in what to do and what not to do. In many institutions, however, there are no such resources other than the psychiatric and social case work staffs and, therefore, there may be a real difficulty in translating understandings so that minister and other workers really talk to each other about the patient's welfare rather than about their own anxieties in figuring out where each stands in relationship to the other.

It is not within the scope of this book to attempt to give guidelines as to how to handle conversation with disturbed people, with or without the guidance of a trained chaplain or a psychiatric staff with some appreciation of the pastor's role. It is important to point out the problems as questions to be taken seriously, to be lived with, to be handled in the best way possible depending on the resources available. Behind and beyond all that is done is the basic premise: the patient in the mental hospital is also a child of God whom the fellowship of the Holy People will not forget.

Whatever form the emotional breakdown may take, the average institutional patient tends to wonder whether anybody outside the hospital itself cares whether he lives or dies, gets well or stays sick. Whether this is complicated by extreme problems of guilt or feelings of basic inadequacy to meet life's demands or unsolved conflicts with parents, partners or children is something to be explored with the hospital staff. In any event, the pastor's concern, even when it has little tangible result, can be a vital resource in the patient's recovery. At the same time, every concerned and knowledgeable minister has to recognize that there will be instances when the patient will project his problem on the Church and often on the minister as the agent of the Church, and then the pastoral role may best be served by not calling except on the advice of the hospital. Yet he still remembers the patient in his prayers and waits for the opportunity to be more directly concerned.

The Ministry to General Hospitals

Very little has been said in this chapter on the ministry to those in general hospitals, because in one sense such a treatment would require a whole book in itself, and in another sense what has been said about the chronically ill and those in mental institutions also applies to those with emergency illnesses and undergoing operations. The minister as the focus of the supporting love of the Holy People of God is concerned not to let people wall themselves off in lonely isolation, conscious chiefly of their own suffering.

One of the aspects of the ministry to those in general hospitals, which might receive some attention here, is the problem of fear. While fear and anxiety certainly are components of most situations involving the chronically ill and shut-ins, they are more often general and pervasive or just additional symptoms of the chronic condition. Again, these problems are certainly involved in most situations of emotional breakdown, but here they are part of the total symptomatology and are being dealt with as such. In many situations involving emergency illness—a coronary attack, or ulcers, or an impending operation, such as a hysterectomy or on the digestive tract—the patient is confronted with a sense of possible doom, which is not necessarily part of his illness as such, but rather the result of being aware that he is ill without being sure how it will come out.

It is not the pastor's role to impart medical information to the patient even when the pastor himself knows. It is not the pastor's responsibility to promise definite medical developments as the probable result of treatment. It is his task to communicate God's answer to fear—*Perfect love casteth out fear.* The curse of fear is not the uncertainty as to the outcome, even though it often appears to center precisely at this point, but rather that one is alone and forgotten, and therefore may be lost and gone forever. The answer, therefore, to the underlying basis of fear—unsureness as to the meaningfulness of one's own life—is the love of the God who cares, who shares our miseries with us, who walks through every valley where we have to go, and this love is made manifest through the patient support of the pastor, whose prayers and counsel are friendly, loving, supportive and above all concerned for the patient as a person.

Dealing with the problem of fear cannot help but raise the question of Christian responsibility to the dying, particularly in those situations where the medical staff feel that the patient ought not to be told his true plight. Again, it is not the pastor's responsibility to by-pass the medical staff's duties, even though he can and sometimes must raise these questions directly with the doctors themselves. It is true that where patients give up hope, they do not have sufficient will to make the best use of what is being done for them. It is also true that doctors are sometimes embarrassed by the imminence of a patient's death, not so much for the patient's welfare—he may be able to take it better than the doctor—but because they do not know what to say nor how to tell one who trusts them that this trust is in vain. In any event, within the limits of possibility, it is the task of the pastor to help those who are dying to accept the love of a God who will not let them go even when they pass over "the great divide." While obviously he cannot give any picture of what is on the other side, he can share a confident faith *that neither death, nor life . . . shall be able to separate us from the love of God . . .*

The Communion of the Sick

Bringing the Holy Communion to the sick not only serves the same purpose that providing the sacrament does for persons in any situation, but it also emphasizes most dramatically what the general ministry to the sick is trying to do. Not every sick call involves bringing the Holy Communion to the patient, of course. But in those circumstances where it is the appropriate occasion for the visit, the meaning of all calls on the sick is highlighted.

In my own pastoral practice, bread and wine are reserved at a regular Sunday service at a time when they are consecrated for the communions of those who are in church. These elements are invariably used for the communion of the sick. If the patient has not previously received the Holy Communion apart from the regularly stated services in the church building, the process is explained to him in order that he may understand himself to be participating sacramentally not only in the life of the Mystical Body of Christ but also in the ongoing existence of that unit of God's Holy People to which he belongs, or indeed which seeks to include him in its fellowship. Because the circumstances of his illness prevent him from attending with the congregation before the altar, the Church symbolically comes to him with the same sacramental elements of bread and wine and includes him in its self-offering to God and its corporate acceptance of the new life in Christ.

Through the sacrament of the Holy Communion the Church reaches out to identify itself concretely with those of its members who need its special concern. God's loving concern is made manifest in dynamically dramatic form. It has been my own pastoral practice to seek out those who are sick and shut in immediately following Christmas and Easter, even though they may not have requested to receive the Holy Communion brought to them, because they will realize that those who are able to go to church will be receiving the Holy Communion at these sacred times. Indeed, I believe that the sacrament should be brought on the days immediately following the high festivals, and that the minister cannot believe his observance of the holidays to be completed until this is done. Those who would have been present if they had been able are thus included in the Church's experience of an encounter in love with the Lord of the Church.

One useful and effective way by which sick and shut-in people can know that the concern of the Christian Fellowship is more than the personal sympathetic interest of the minister is for a lay person or two to accompany the priest bringing Communion. While in some situations—as immediately after a major operation or where there is serious emotional disturbance—this may not be desirable, in the majority of circumstances it is both practicable and very helpful. The Communion is administered, as the Church has always meant it to be, within the worshipping congregation. The patient is told, without anyone saying so in words, that in the presence and power of Christ isolation is broken through.

Along with the special emphasis on bringing the Holy Communion to every sick and shut-in person who can be reached on the days immediately following Christmas and Easter, there is a general value in making this ministration available throughout the year. Sometimes people will request it. In many situations it provides the best possible spiritual preparation for an operation, provided there is a background of understanding between pastor and parishioner. In many situations, the offer of the sacrament will prove to be that type of pastoral concern which brings peace and power to those who have been shut out.

CHAPTER VIII

THE MINISTRY

TO THE BEREAVED

Every Christian congregation expects that one of the continuing responsibilities of its minister will be the conducting of funerals. Even in new suburban communities, largely peopled by young couples, death strikes every now and then and the Church has to be prepared to handle it.

It is one thing, however, to provide for the reverent disposal of the remains of someone who has died, and quite another thing to provide an adequate ministry for those who are bereaved. This ministry is a most important part of the general field of pastoral care, and more attention needs to be given to the meaning and purpose of what is done. The prevailing pattern of funeral customs in many communities tends to concentrate so much on the deceased that the bereaved are made secondary and dealt with in sentimental formalities.

One of the tasks of the pastoral ministry, therefore, is to help reverse values in situations where this is called for. In every mainstream tradition of Christendom something akin to the phrase, "Unto Almighty God we commit the soul of our brother (sister) departed," is said, yet the tone of the proceedings does not really suggest that people

98

mean it. As Christians we trust God to take care of those who have passed beyond this life—indeed there is nothing else that we can do that has any real meaning. We sometimes fail to give adequate emphasis to the other side of the committal: God commits to his Church on earth the care of the bereaved, because they are the people who need human help here and now.

The ministry to the bereaved is certainly an area in which a shared pastoral ministry can function with great effectiveness, provided it is understood by all who participate—clergymen and laymen—that not everybody is an equally good resource in every aspect of every situation. The layman's role in sensitive acts of brotherly supportiveness may often speak with greater clarity than a thousand books. At the same time, in a peculiarly significant sense the lay sharer in the pastorate may find that his own sense of guilt, as well as of his inadequacy, may be increased by what he finds; and he can easily be tempted to let the bereaved person down too easily just to get himself off the hook. The ordained pastor, because he is human, will find precisely the same problems, but his training may enable him to live with this without letting it confuse his ministry; and he does have a priestly role to perform representing God's forgiveness in the fellowship of his Church.

While the laity may perform a real and vital pastoral service in supporting the bereaved with their concern during the long pull which follows the funeral, the ordained minister cannot expect that anyone but himself will suffice at the deathbed (except in emergency), and in raising the religious significance of the decisions which have to be made in planning funerals. Certainly his relationship—even with relative strangers—is one of privilege; but it is a solemn, responsible privilege which allows a man, even if he is ordained, to be part of someone else's family when they stand at life's frontier.

Every encounter a clergyman has with those whom he is trying to serve in the name of Christ involves a judgment on the quality of his pastoral ministry. This is particularly true in situations which have come to a head, because then it becomes apparent whether or not people are able to meet their problems in the sure confidence that they are part of the supporting, loving fellowship of God's Holy People. While it is true that men and women are often given a grace and courage beyond what we may have any right to expect on the basis of the little that we have done for them and with them, the fact remains that our own ministry is exposed to ourselves if to no one else. Again, while it is true that God does not expect his servants in the ranks of the ordained clergy to "bat a thousand," but rather to depend upon his acceptance and forgiveness and love for them as well as for those they serve, still he does not expect them to find alibis for their shortcomings.

While what has just been said is true about every pastoral situation, it is particularly evident when the clergyman tries to minister in situations where a death has occurred. The moments of immediate crisis are not occasions for reflective teaching. People have to do the best they can with the resources they have already obtained, and while the pastor can do a great deal through friendly support and guidance, he can hardly reorient life's meaning for them while they are in shock. Certainly the pastor will have a tremendous opportunity for his ministry to persons in the days of readjustment following the funeral, but he cannot expect people who are reacting to an immediate death of someone close to them to make decisions on the basis of a faith they never knew.

It is also true that the universal fact of death calls in question the effectiveness of the Church's missionary outreach in the local scene; it also provides sensitive and alert pastors with an opportunity, through their ministry to the bereaved after the funeral, to make contact with people who have been only on the fringes of the Church's life, if even that close. Clergymen are called in when deaths occur, even in families which have only the most tenuous of church connections, because somehow or other it seems fitting that a minister perform the final rites. This may be the result of prevailing social custom, or the heritage of earlier generations which once knew the Church as the context in which life's joys and sorrows are met; but whatever the reason, the situation arises frequently. In these circumstances the pastor cannot expect those who ask his help to have much of an understanding of what he really is there to provide. He can only do the best he can at the time, and look forward to building more creatively upon it afterwards. In all realism, however, a minister needs to recognize that people under the stress of immediate emotional upheaval, such as so often happens when death occurs, may suggest a receptivity to the Church's concern which will not continue after the immediate stress has passed. Yet in every situation where death occurs, there is an opportunity for the pastoral ministry to try to reach the hearts of those concerned.

Funeral Arrangements

The ministry to the bereaved cannot be completely separated from some consideration of funeral customs. While this discussion is not about techniques and methods, it nevertheless stands to reason that there is a real interaction between what people mean and what people do. Where the pastoral relationship with a family is sufficiently meaningful for the pastor to be called before the undertaker—indeed to be called if someone is dying— the Church's part in what is happening will have a better chance to become clear. But men and women do not know that this is what the Church expects them to do unless they are told, and even then they need some help in appreciating what difference it makes. In this, as in many other areas, the teaching ministry and the pastoral ministry complement each other as each makes the other more significant.

While death is in many ways a completely lonely experience for the person who dies, and that kind of encounter with reality for those close to the deceased which is very difficult to share with anyone else, still basic Christian teaching is that we live and die within the fellowship of God's Holy People, and even at life's extremity God's love supports us. If the role of the pastor is seen to be more than that of a friendly, experienced guide—as the representative of that fellowship which exists on earth to be the bearer of God's loving concern for his children—then his attendance in times like these says something both symbolic and powerful. In Christian tradition, regardless of differences of interpretation and emphasis, we pass from the Church Militant—the company of the faithful people of God on earth dealing with the problems of history—to the Church Expectant—the company of God's people in his keeping who await his final consummation of his sovereign divine purpose. We cannot see beyond the curtain, but we trust the same love which sustains us on this side to be with them on the other side, and eventually to support us on our own final pilgrimage. The minister's participation in the whole process of the event of death speaks to this essential Christian faith in a language more meaningful than words.

Again, this discussion is not primarily one of methods, yet they cannot be disregarded here. Where the funeral service takes place in the church building, it obviously, although not automatically, becomes the act of the congregation of God's Holy People in a way impossible in a funeral home. If the service is one of participation of the congregation, the fact that it is the act of God's Holy People, and not an exercise conducted by a minister, comes clear. Psalms can be read responsively. The Apostles' Creed and the Lord's Prayer at least can be said in unison. Where it is possible, one or more triumphant hymns can be sung. The Church lays to rest one of its own, and sustains with its triumphant corporate faith those who remain. But such an approach to death and funerals will not happen unless the pastoral relationship has had some meaning beforehand.

The pastoral ministry can have a great deal to do, as it supplements the teaching ministry through face-to-face discussion, with the eradication of a morbid, sentimental feeling about the body of the deceased. God gave us human bodies to use in life, not just for ourselves but for others as well, through acts of service. It is quite within God's loving purpose for us to carry this on even through death. There is nothing irreverent about an autopsy which may add to the fund of medical knowledge, and thus help other sufferers in the long run. There is nothing irreverent about arranging with hospitals to take those "spare parts," so to speak—corneas, skin, bones, ligaments, which can be salvaged for helping others to health. Perhaps it is better for the deceased to have made these arrangements himself earlier, but whether or not this has been done, the provision of these parts is no discourtesy to the body of the deceased but rather an extension of charity beyond mortal life.

There will be many occasions when the pastor will be asked his opinion as to the relative merits of cremation versus interment of the body. As a human being he will of course have opinions, even though he may not feel them very strongly. The Church, however, has no opinion—in the sense that one custom has more religious meaning than the other. The body should be disposed of in a dignified manner because God gave it and now its original usefulness is past. Families need help in not going overboard in making provision for the disposal of the body— expensive caskets, many flowers, and other forms of display.

In many congregations the use of a pall—a beautifully embroidered cloth to cover the casket in a way similar to the use of the flag for a veteran—has come to be the accepted pattern. The pall serves several valuable purposes, suggesting that it is not necessary to compete with others in floral blankets because the Church, as God's Holy People, treats all her children alike. Again, the teaching and pastoral ministries serve each other at this point.

The Ministry to Grief

When the clergyman seeks to minister to grief, he does not wait to be consulted. He assumes that the problem is there because of his knowledge of human nature. And while some people may hide their grief behind a kind of modern stoicism, and others may have their grief compounded with a sense of relief that an ordeal is over, nevertheless there is usually confusion in the face of life's ultimate questions, and people need to talk.

The pastor need not wait to be asked. He will normally call at the homes of those who have asked him to conduct a funeral, both before the services and within a week afterwards. Whether the particular form of counseling that is called for in bereavement will be carried on in the living room or in his study will depend on circumstances. His own sensitivity to people will tell him which to suggest. In many situations he will expect to have a series of conferences.

In the ministry to the bereaved, the clergyman will encounter three aspects of the problem of grief in nearly every situation. Sometimes one will be more intense than the other two, and sometimes one will appear to be so minor as to be insignificant. But in nearly every case all three aspects will be in the picture in one form or another. These are: guilt, sense of loss, and the reminder of one's own eventual death. While this writer would expect the order given to describe their relative importance in most situations, this would not necessarily always be the case. On the other hand, he would expect to explore all three with gentleness so that if they were not immediately apparent even to the bereaved, they could still be dealt with if there were reason for so doing.

Guilt is a very important factor in the grief people feel when someone close to them has died, even though they may not be ready or willing to accept the reality without some help. Despite what people say, there have been raw spots in every intimate relationship. In every close association, feelings have been hurt at least once in awhile, and resentments have been carried. When the surviving partner in a marriage says, "There never was an angry word between us," whom is he trying to fool? Perhaps he may be correct as far as words go, but how about feelings? In any event, the fact of death draws a line across the relationship exactly as it happens to be with all that has gone before, and there it is—an unchangeable fact of history.

If a long protracted illness has preceded the death,

there may be additional reasons for guilt, because few patients undergo long illnesses without showing some effects on the level of personality. They become unreasonable in their demands, or querulous, or noncommunicative, or even exasperatingly noble; and those who care for them cannot help feeling some resentment at the time, even though they may understand why the patients react as they do. When death occurs, the survivors remember these resentments and feel unhappy about them. Again, a long illness may have been rather expensive, and the family will not have been altogether happy about reorganizing its financial resources to meet the pressure; and once more people feel guilty, this time for having been grudging.

A most poignant aspect of the problem of guilt is the feeling people frequently have that if somehow they had acted differently, the death itself would not have occurred. More often than not people know that this feeling cannot be justified by the facts, but they still feel it. My mother, for instance, felt very badly after my father had died as a result of a coronary attack, because she had not been more alert for symptoms. Even if she had had a medical education and knew that a coronary attack was a possibility, it still could have occurred without warning and turned out to be fatal. People also torture themselves for having taken a trip and therefore not immediately available when wanted, or they may blame themselves for having brought up some unpleasant subject for discussion.

The very fact that we feel that, somehow or other, we have contributed to the demise of someone for whom we have responsibility says something which cannot be dealt with simply by arguing the objective facts pro and con. Our relationships are always incomplete. We know in our hearts that we have a share of responsibility for the problems that made life hard for others.

Regardless of the details surrounding the actual dying, death rarely finds a relationship with all the strings tied together. The apology which perhaps should have been made can no longer be offered because it cannot be received. The kindness which might have been repaid is left hanging in the air. The appreciation which was never quite fully expressed is turned backward on the one who failed to act. Death writes *finis,* and we are caught where we are. In no other way does life teach us the reality of our own moral fallibility as well as when death strikes close to home. Regardless of the words people may use, they are forced to recognize, at least to some little extent, that they cannot be their own redeemers because the relationship is beyond their power to handle, once death has taken away one of the members.

When death strikes, men and women are caught in the reality of guilt without possibility of real escape. Here then is the chance to make effective the Gospel proclamation that God accepts us because we are his children, not because we have been perfect; that God forgives us because he cares; and in his saving life, death, and resurrection Jesus Christ shares the depth of the human problem, so that all he asks is for us to confess our sin and receive what is so freely offered; and that God loves us now and forever.

Along with the fact of guilt is the problem of loss and separation. In many instances our sense of guilt will add to our sense of loss, because it will mean that we cannot restore what is incomplete; but separation has some significance in its own right. People need each other to be themselves, and to the extent that our lives are seriously involved in the lives of other people we are deprived of part of our own selfhood by their going. John Donne was quite right when he said:

Any man's death diminishes me, because I am involved in mankind; And therefore never send to know for whom the bell tolls; It tolls for thee.

Where there is grief involving a sense of loss, there is no point in acting as if the loss were not real. It is real, and the separation is a fact. Most men and women are not helped particularly by being told that there will be a reuniting at some later date "on the far, distant shore." The loss is now, and one's life is that much incomplete as the result of it. The pastoral ministry, however, has very real resources to bring to those who feel this pain, and these can be talked over quietly, and over a period of time.

The first necessary step to handling the problem of loss is admitting the finality of what has happened. The death is not a sham but a reality. The writer of this book had this brought home to him with particular force after he had officiated at the reinterment of American servicemen brought home to local cemeteries from Europe and Asia. My first reaction to the idea that these men be brought back was to feel that this was silly, wasteful, and useless; but when they were returned and the families saw the caskets lowered into the ground, the survivors seemed better able to accept what had happened and to turn their faces toward the future. In many older traditions there has been the custom of having the close relatives each throw a shovelful of earth on the casket at the interment—a custom which modern Americans have discarded as being crude and painful. As a matter of fact, in those situations where I have seen this done because family custom demanded it, the result has been therapeutic. In any event, regardless of the symbolism involved, there is no healing possible until the reality of death and separation has been admitted to be what it is. Certainly it is unchristian and deceitful for a minister to use rose petals rather than earth at the committal.

After accepting facts for facts, there is then the possibility of providing a new orientation in which to live with reality. Christian experience has insisted, from New Testament times until the present, that the closer people are to Christ the nearer they are to each other. During World War II a number of servicemen wrote to me from various theaters of combat to say how they felt the miles and the months bridged by attending the service of the Holy Communion. This is even more true where death has occurred. We are close to those we love as we are close to Christ. Communion is a sharing of God's loving gift of life not only with those who are attending the service with us at the moment, but with the total Church in the world and beyond. In the Book of Common Prayer, the celebration of the Holy Communion, in the technical sense, begins with the prayer for Christ's Church, associating the worshippers with all Christian folk who are in God's care. The American revision of 1928 eliminated the word "militant," which would limit the prayer for the Church to living Christians and added an intercession for those who have died. These liturgical devices serve the purpose of making overt what Christian faith has always known. While we may not see through the curtain, we know God's love to be equally real on both sides.

Finally, there is no denying that in many instances grief is strongly colored by the reminder to the bereaved that he, too, will die. In many situations this aspect of the problem will be only semi-conscious, but in others it will be quite clear. In any event, the concerned pastor needs gently to explore this side of the feelings of those he seeks to help. It is both psychologically and spiritually desirable that this aspect be dealt with, except where circumstances force it to the forefront of the counseling discussion after the problems of guilt and loss have been faced. This is because what the Christian faith has to say about the first two aspects of grief becomes the precondition for what it has to say about the third.

The fear of death is in many ways man's most universal anxiety. It takes a variety of forms depending upon custom, tradition and experience, and is in itself more symbolic than actual. It exists whether or not there has been a bereavement, but the death of someone close may remind us of the incomplete nature of our coming to terms with our own eventual decease. Has life any meaning other than what we as human beings put into it and maintain? If it has no such meaning, then death is the end of the world for us. Can we live honestly with our unsolved problems and only half-fulfilled relationships? If we see no focus here, then death threatens to wipe out everything that matters.

It is not surprising that one of the dreams which occurs in so many people's experience, as to be almost universal, is the fear of being buried alive. This dream, regardless of details, usually has the dreamer conscious of his predicament, and it seems to suggest a hopeless isolation from all meaning. There is no point to existence, and the dreamer is lost beyond recovery—out of contact with any other person's concern, beyond even the care of the Most High God.

In many ways what has been said here will become the subject matter of counseling interviews where the cause

has nothing to do with bereavement. But it is true that our grief over the death of someone close to us can remind us of our own mortality and bring our natural anxiety to the forefront of consciousness. The way the pastor deals with this fear of death in his counseling will depend upon a great many factors, and no generalization will be very helpful. The basis of the Church's way of handling this problem, however, is to reassure troubled people that they are important; that God cares; that this care is not simply theory but a living fact; that God's Holy People serve on earth to reinforce the significance of every person's life; and the clergy themselves have the function of focusing these truths.

CHAPTER IX

THE CHRISTIAN FAITH
AND PROBLEMS OF MARRIAGE

Everybody who cares at all about the function of the Christian Church in the modern world accepts the fact that there is an intimate connection between the pastoral ministry and family life. Such phrases as "The Church is the Family of Families," and "The Family is the Little Church within the Church" are commonly used in describing this relationship even though there is not always very much deep thought given to the implications of these phrases. Because family life, involving husbands and wives and parents and children, is the norm of society—single people, unmarried or widowed, are the exceptions despite any questions of mathematical proportion—it is obvious that the Church must have a significant ministry to every phase of family living, if it is to be relevant in the modern world.

People take for granted that the Church is involved in the conduct of marriages, even though this is more often than not regarded as maintaining the institution which sees to the arrangements. The basic truth, however, is that men and women who seek to tell each other and the world that their relationship to each other is made, as it were, in heaven use the forms which society and con-

vention demand and make available as the means of demonstrating that "the knot is tied." The Church has a continual task in helping those who come to be married to appreciate the deeper meaning of the setting which they wish to use for the rite. This is a responsibility of both the educational and pastoral aspects of the Church's life.

When people have marital difficulties, however, they often look for help—at least in the initial stages—and within limits are willing to ask for assistance from any reasonable source. More often than not they do not turn to the Church, largely because they do not expect it to have very much to offer in the area of their concern. Again, part of the continuing responsibility of both the educational and pastoral aspects of the Church's life is to provide ways and means of telling people that the Christian Church is meant to be the framework within which they face their conflicts, even though they may often need the assistance of such specialized services as psychiatry, gynecology, and social case work in the course of understanding what is involved.

The pastoral ministry to the problems of marriage involves the minister both as the person whose sacerdotal and quasi-legal offices are required in having any service in the Church at all, and even more as counselor and teacher in the whole process of preparation. But the minister does not stand alone, even though by both ecclesiastical and civil law he has certain privileges which cannot be shared. In a general sense, the tone of the congregational life, as evidenced by the way married couples share functionally in the Church's ministry to its own and to the world, provides a pastoral and educational pattern which is much more effective than thousands of words. In a more specific sense, the laity can have a real share even in the liturgical aspects of preparation for marriage. Cer-

tainly through discussion groups and special classes the Church's teaching about the nature of marriage can be made the common resource of all its members—and this means something more than lectures by the ordained minister.

Again, while the minister in his professional capacity —along with such skilled partners as the psychiatrist, the gynecologist and the social worker—may have to operate directly, the climate in which these problems are faced, if they are met in a Christian way, cannot be created by the clergyman alone. The Church as the Holy Fellowship ministers to its troubled members by providing an atmosphere in which forgiveness is taken seriously in the name of the Lord, because guilt is not ducked but faced. Within this setting, there is room for the psychiatrist, the gynecologist, and the social caseworker to discover for themselves not only a human ministry to troubled people, but a kind of priesthood in the name of the Most High God. But even if the particular people with these skills never sense this dimension of their vocation, the Church's understanding still can give these skills a religious significance.

Preparation for Marriage

The Christian Church has an ambiguous relationship to the conduct of weddings. Many people, in spite of the fact that they may have only the vaguest understanding of what the Church exists to do, still believe that marriages should be conducted under Church auspices, yet they are often surprised when they find that the minister is not primarily concerned with where the bridesmaids shall stand and what kind of flowers are on the altar, but rather that he is vitally interested in the maturity with which the young man and woman are approaching the new relationship.

There is much to be said for the European custom which requires that all marriages be performed by the civil authorities—at the registry or the mayor's office—with a religious ceremony taking place only where people go to the trouble to ask for something not required at law. Too often the fact that the clergy are used as ordained notaries, supervising the establishment of a contract at law, confuses the issue both as to marriage itself and as to the role of the Church. It is the task of the pastoral ministry to prepare people to meet reality in every form; and the marriage relationship is one of the most basic there is. In the course of dedicating the commitment a man and a woman make to each other, the clergyman is also called upon to give advice as to the pattern of the ceremony in much the same manner that some people buy copies of Emily Post.

While a beautiful and dignified wedding service is certainly to be desired, the pastor's task is primarily in the preparation of the couple for marriage and in seeing that there is a continuing relationship with the Church afterwards, in which what has been promised will receive the support of the larger fellowship. Without this kind of structure, marriage is solely a matter of the good intentions and ethical standards of the people concerned, undergirded by the prevailing social mores.

Many books have been written about counseling in preparation for marriage. The only point to be noted here is that there is a unique opportunity in the course of preparing young people for marriage to make the great theological insights of the Christian faith relevant in the most dynamic possible way. The word *faith* is so often taken to be a list of opinions to which one is supposed to adhere, rather than the conviction upon which one gambles his life. When a young couple get married, they do not know

the future. We hope they will use their best intelligence as well as avail themselves of the guidance of others in every possible area—yet they will not know the future. If this marriage is to be a reality, they must act as if it were "made in heaven," even though they cannot prove it.

Again, marriage provides a wonderful setting for appreciating the deeper meaning of forgiveness and grace. No two people can share a life and agree one hundred per cent of the time. No two people can build plans together, and accept responsibilities involving each other, without at least occasionally taking advantage of each other and having their feelings hurt. One of the questions I always ask in my own marriage counseling is, "Have you known each other long enough to have faced any serious disagreements and, if so, how did you handle them?" Sometimes the young couple seem confused, as if they felt that the minister would disapprove of them if they admitted having any conflict, when the reverse is true. Only some experience in handling hostility can indicate whether people are ready to accept the responsibility of marriage.

The ministry of pastoral care and the teaching ministry of the Church support each other in a most valuable way. Conducting a rehearsal can be a tremendously valuable pastoral opportunity. My own practice is to make the required signing of legal documents a solemn occasion in the presence of the entire wedding party, including parents, after which the rehearsal itself begins with prayer, followed by an interpretation of the meaning of the marriage service in the Book of Common Prayer, paragraph by paragraph. I believe that it is most important for the young couple to memorize their own vows—indeed it is theologically inaccurate for them to parrot them back to a clergyman, whose voice is most often the only one heard by the congregation. The officiating ministers at the

wedding are the bride and the groom. The clergyman is the official witness who performs his religious task by dedicating these vows with prayer and blessing. Young people can be helped to see their relationship before God by understanding why things should be done this way.

Birth Control

Sometimes in the course of his premarital conferences a clergyman will be asked to give his opinion on birth control. Whether or not the young couple bring it up, it is his solemn obligation to explore this issue with them. Much has been written in this area from the technical standpoint, and it is certainly his task to see that people are placed in contact with those who can give them adequate counsel on this level. My own practice is to require every couple to read a book on the biology of marriage and for the girl, at least, to counsel with a reputable gynecologist.

The clergyman's primary responsibility is to deal with the theology of birth control. People do have doubts. Even the Twentieth Century has yet to dispose of superstitious fears. There is a kind of vague, pervasive feeling that sex is wrong except where the birth of children is a direct possibility. Even well educated men and women are confused as to the function of sex in establishing a dynamic symbol of their relationship to each other.

In the Episcopal Church every couple is required to sign the following statement before a marriage takes place:

We, * * * desiring to receive the blessing of Holy Matrimony in the Church, do solemnly declare that we hold marriage to be a lifelong union of husband and wife as it is set forth in the Form of Solemnization of Holy Matrimony in the Book of Common Prayer.

We believe it is for the purpose of mutual fellowship,

117

encouragement, and understanding, for the procreation (if it may be) of children, and their physical and spiritual nurture, for the safeguarding and benefit of society.

And we do engage ourselves, so far as in us lies, to make our utmost effort to establish this relationship and to seek God's help thereto.

The foregoing is only one side of the problem. Another side is answering effectively the kind of thing which characterizes the Roman Catholic attitude: the confused distinction between natural and artificial, and the equally confused ideas about abusing freedom.

Every scientific discovery from Salk vaccine to atomic fission is the result of God's gift. On the one hand, the discovery could not be made unless, within God's providence, that which was found was already there. On the other hand, neither could the discovery be made unless God had given his children the capacity for finding it. There is nothing intrinsically artificial about scientific birth control under the competent guidance of a physician. It is on the same level as vaccination and wearing eye glasses.

God gave his children the capacity for sex not merely that the race might survive, but just as much in order that they might meet each other as persons in the fullest and most meaningful way. A young couple does need children, if it is humanly possible to bring them into the world, because the love of a man for a woman becomes ingrown in many instances unless it can be expressed on some third person who is the symbol of the love that they have for each other. As the "only child" will bear fervent witness, families need more than one child (again if it is humanly possible) in order to save the child from the awkwardness of being the one junior in the family.

When all this is said, however, the question still remains to be handled as to how many children a family should have and how far apart they should come. These questions should not be answered in a doctrinaire manner. It is not the Church's task to give specific guidance here. It is the Church's task to insist that people in all conscience use their intelligence in so planning their relationships that the best welfare of all concerned is protected. If children come too close together, or there are too many, it may interfere with the mother's health or it may prejudice the economic stability of the family. Different people, however, will deal with these questions in different ways. The Church's responsibility is to see that they are dealt with as intelligently as possible and without any old wives' tales or primitive superstitions masking under the name of the Christian faith.

It is my own practice to insist that adequate instruction be received from a competent gynecologist. I feel so strongly about this that I would not knowingly perform a marriage ceremony where people had failed to get this instruction. I would feel that the burden of proof would be on the couple as to whether they were sufficiently mature to be married at all, if they were irresponsible in this basic area; and my judgment would be on theological grounds quite as much as on scientific and sociological ones. In telling a young couple about this, I always make it clear that the Church will not tell them when and how to use the information they have received. This is a matter for conscience in the light of all the reality factors. The Church, however, cannot allow them to be irresponsible without its being irresponsible. To be sure, sexual intercourse can be as much a form of self-indulgence as are a great many other things.

The fact that one of God's gifts can be abused does not

destroy its original value. The same would be true about driving an automobile. Where God has enabled us to manufacture internal combustion engines and hitch them to wheels, he has also given us the ability to navigate these vehicles on the highways. This does not mean, however, that they will be driven carefully just because they exist. Every gift of God is used under his judgment and by his grace. This does not prevent failure, but it may mean serious confusion as the result of irresponsible use. Men can and do pervert what God has made available, but this does not mean that they must be protected against their own freedom. After all, the administration of the Church itself is in the hands of human beings who are just as likely to take advantage of their moral authority over men's souls as other men are over their physical capacity to use people's bodies.[1]

Marital Difficulty

Every minister who has acquired any reputation for being approachable and keeping confidences will be asked for help in situations where marriages are either on the rocks or undergoing serious difficulty. Regardless of how much special skill he may have in this type of problem, he will be asked anyhow, because the situation arises so fre-

---

[1] Resolution 115 of *The Lambeth Conference 1958* (p. 157) says: "The Conference believes that the responsibility for deciding upon the number and frequency of children has been laid by God upon the consciences of parents everywhere: that this planning, in such ways as are mutually acceptable to husband and wife in Christian conscience, is a right and important factor in Christian family life and should be the result of positive choice before God. Such responsible parenthood, built on obedience to all the duties of marriage, requires a wise stewardship of the resources and abilities of the family as well as a thoughtful consideration of the varying population needs and problems of society and the claims of future generations."

quently in modern American urban society. While much of what has been said in the chapter on Pastoral Counseling applies here, there are some special points which may well be made.

Comparative statistics on the divorce rate are not particularly important except as a straw in the wind. It is true that divorces are easier to obtain in many States, both because of legislation and of the way the laws are interpreted; and it is also true that divorce does not involve the social stigma it once did. Any pastor, however, who has done much work with people in marital difficulty knows that there is a high degree of accident involved in determining which cases get to the divorce court. Where help has been procured early enough, people have often found a way to work through their problems creatively, and have been assisted in growing up sufficiently to be more realistic in their expectations both of their partners and themselves. Those who get this help are, first, those who are led to seek it and, secondly, those who become open enough to use it. But it does not follow that just because a couple seeks guidance in dealing with marital conflict, they will necessarily arrive at a happy solution. Yet many of the cases which do end in the courts could have been helped if the people concerned had known that help was available, how to find it, and had been helped to use it.

Marriage is of the order of creation. Christian marriage is of the order of redemption. These theological statements are basic to any effective Christian pastorate to marital problems. Men and women in every social system will mate according to the patterns that system decrees, both to procreate the species and because male and female are necessary to each other for the fulfillment of personality. But it is one thing to marry, even according to the wisest counsel that modern western society has developed, and quite another thing to discover what Christian marriage means. Christian marriage involves discovering, through God's help, the real meaning of acceptance, forgiveness and mature love—as a man and a woman make decisions, work through conflicts, and share a life which will never be roses without thorns. The pastoral ministry to marital problems is primarily a business of bringing to the light of a faith which is loving rather than rigid the misunderstandings and hurts which tear people's hearts and make them afraid to be more than strangers to each other.

Involved in marital difficulties are a variety of factors: sexual, relations with in-laws and parents, economic, clashes over likes and dislikes, and so on. Often special skills, such as those of the psychiatrist, the marriage counselor, the gynecologist with a psychiatric orientation, or the social caseworker, are needed or at least can be very helpful. These resources do not eliminate the need for the specifically Christian insight into marriage, but they are most valuable in making marriage viable, as understood within the order of creation (as a natural phenomenon). Along with these most helpful resources is the Christian note that conflict is not, in and of itself, ultimately destructive—Christian marriage is not a relationship without disagreements and problems—but acceptance and forgiveness make it possible for people to meet as persons in the presence of God.

Those who come to the pastor for help do not, as a rule, need to be told that more is involved than their own individual feelings. Besides the feelings of the other party is also the welfare of the children. Perhaps the minister, as any other counselor, through patient, non-judgmental questions, may help sharpen the awareness of the counselee in this area so that he looks at his total situation in so far as possible. But the minister will seek to avoid adding to the guilt this person already feels, even though he may be trying to hide from it by projecting on his partner the major responsibility for the difficulty. Certainly the welfare of the children has a kind of priority over the convenience and desires of their parents, yet the parents are still people with lives to live. God cares for them in their own right, but he expects an adequate discharge of their parental responsibility.

The survival of any particular marriage, however, is not, in and of itself, to be regarded as good, with divorce as the absolute evil. There are situations where the pastor has to admit that an end to an intolerable relationship will be best for all concerned. Perhaps this is not his decision to make, as if he were the final authority; but, on the other hand, it is not his duty to block divorce on formalistic grounds just because he disapproves of marriages ever breaking up. Certainly there is a tremendous responsibility to be faced before accepting divorce as the best solution, as the end of a marriage is not to be taken lightly even where the welfare of children is not a problem. The survival of a particular relationship which does not change or improve—even though endless trouble has been taken and people have tried as conscientiously as they could—such a survival is condemning men and women to hell. While marriage is of the order of God's creation, like other natural institutions it was made for man, not the other way round. The pastor sometimes is the only one who can help people accept these realities without assuming in the process an intolerable load of guilt.

The ministry to marital difficulty involves also pastoral care for those who have been divorced, often without benefit of counsel from the Church, even though they may have had other kinds of help in trying to save their marriages. In many situations, the sense of relief experienced after a divorce is accompanied by a sense of failure which grows with the passing days. This is particularly true of women, although men know it too, and both men and women try to hide it from the world and even from themselves. Failure in marriage, however, is not the unforgivable sin. Certainly it is unfortunate. Even though predominant blame may be placed by an impartial third party more on one person than the other, in any relationship there will be some real cause for guilt in the experience of both parties. The pastoral ministry of acceptance and forgiveness within God's Holy People can be most important in making it possible for these people to recover a sense of personal value.

CHAPTER X

CHRISTIAN FAITH
AND PROBLEMS OF
SOCIAL ASSISTANCE

The ministry of pastoral care may include a number of relationships with people, both those officially connected with the congregation and those coming to him from the community, where the basis for the encounter is a request for some tangible form of assistance. While this type of pastoral ministry in many instances will overlap those described in the chapters on counseling and the ministry to the sick, and some situations will arise in the course of pastoral visiting, the fact that there is some form of concrete planning involved requires special attention here. In Chapter IV, we saw how trouble isolates people, and this is just as true of social dislocation as it is of physical illness or emotional breakdown.

The ministry to those who need social assistance clarifies in two significant ways how the ministry of pastoral care cannot be limited to the ordained clergy, yet at the same time lays particular responsibilities upon them. On the one hand, here is an area in which professional social workers, in private and public agencies rather than in the institutional Church, may be helped to find their work not only a professional skill but also a ministry in the name of Christ within the fellowship of the Holy People of God. On the other hand, where official representation of the Church, as such, is involved, special care needs to be taken in order that the function of the Holy People within history will not be obscured—and whether it is lay partners or the minister himself who deal with those asking aid, this point has to be appreciated lest social confusion become the worse confounded. The confidential nature of many situations requiring assistance in most instances seems to indicate that only those with recognized professional responsibility and training—whether clergymen or social workers—become very deeply involved in cases.

Along with such training in personality development and behavior, including insight into himself which will enable the pastor to work more effectively in situations of emotional tension possibly involving referral to or cooperation with psychiatrists, and along with such training in the problems of the sick and aging which will make this side of the pastoral ministry as helpful as possible, the clergyman needs some training in the processes and purposes of social case work. The purpose of this training is not to make him a caseworker, but rather to help him to have some understanding of the diagnostic side of social case work, and also to be able to work in cooperation with the professionals in social agencies.

Many a clergyman is very vague as to the purposes of social case work agencies, and he tends to think of them either as places where problems can be dumped which are not his responsibility when he does not otherwise know how to get rid of them without feeling guilty, or as resources to do the "leg work" in carrying out plans which he believes to be best for the welfare of an individual or a family for which he does have responsibility. Neither side of this picture helps in the kind of cooperation which agencies, clergymen, and the community at large all need if the best interests of people are to be served.

There has been almost a half-century of misunderstanding between professional social workers and clergymen, although there have been many notable exceptions where the most effective cooperation and mutual appreciation have occurred. This situation is increasingly better with the passing years, because there is greater knowledge on the part of the clergy as to what social workers do. At the same time, case work has largely outgrown a kind of mechanistic attitude toward personality and society which, despite good intentions and warm hearts in many workers, made the handling of situations seem to be more the manipulation of things rather than a dealing with personalities.

A major aspect of the problem is that clergymen tend to think of themselves as competent social case workers, who make up for their lack of technical training by what they believe to be a more sincere reverence for the personalities of those they are trying to help. This is usually nothing but sentimentality mixed with a kind of destructive pride, which makes the minister feel that somehow he has failed his parishioner if he has not been able to take the primary responsibility in working through the solution of the problem. The ideal relationship, which is much more than a dream, is one where the clergyman and the professional social worker have sufficient mutual respect for each other, both as persons and as people with special skills, for them to complement each other for the larger welfare of individuals and families in trouble.

In those communities where there are several social welfare agencies with specifically assigned responsibilities, it is important that the minister either know what each is set up to do, or to have the counsel of someone in the professional social work field to advise him on referrals. Endless confusion is caused when agencies are asked to go beyond their functions and when people are referred to resources which are not equipped to help them.

While large cities have a variety of social welfare agencies, and the Public Welfare Department has divisions dealing with the various categories of public assistance established by law in more than three thousand rural communities in America, there is only one agency with whom the minister can cooperate—the local public welfare authority. Whether the minister is working in the complex structure of the large city or in the simpler pattern of the small town, he always needs to have effective contacts with those in the professional social work field. Since social case work is one of God's gifts for the well-being of his children in society, it is entitled to be taken seriously, and functional cooperation is, in its way, a form of reverence.

In some larger communities there have been established committees to help make it possible for the Church and social case work to communicate with each other. Church-sponsored agencies increasingly are accepting the same standards and disciplines that are followed in the most effective community agencies. Clergymen and laymen serve on agency boards where they learn what is going on and why; and at the same time they have an opportunity to make their own influence felt. Seriously concerned clergy, lay volunteers, and professional social workers in a few cities are wrestling with the deeper implications of the theology of social case work, in order that what is done in the areas served by public and private agencies, which usually have very high ethical motivations, will more directly reflect the Christian faith.

Requests for Tangible Assistance

While in some instances social agencies will turn to a clergyman whom they trust, either because of special skill he may have or, better, because of the kind of relationship the client has with the church or its pastor, most situations involving requests for tangible assistance come first to the clergyman and are referred by him, if referral takes place, to the social agencies. People turn to the clergy for this kind of help, because of the reasons given in Chapter IV, and also because they sometimes feel that a relationship with him will be easier and less demanding than with a community resource. Sometimes people come to the clergy for tangible help because they expect him to be a kind of social encyclopedia of what is possible, and sometimes because they think he will be a soft touch.

While the forms of social dislocation which affect men and women who require tangible assistance of some kind can be catalogued in considerable detail, certain basic Christian convictions apply throughout. God is concerned with the total welfare of his children more than he is with their physical and mental health and their sense of belonging to a church. He cares about family relationships, the needs people have for someone to love, or to have someone already loved receive adequate care. God does not regard economic pressures as outside the realm of his concern. As a matter of fact, concerned ministers feel the same way. Yet it is very easy to deal with these problems, whether or not they are referred for special help, as if they were to be handled solely on the level of human arrangements. When human needs are met as if they were chores, even pleasant or attractive ones, it is not the same thing as if the Holy People of God, as representatives of the divine concern, were reaching out to include persons in fellowship. And when people are included seriously, there is room for even their unsolved problems.

While any experienced pastoral counselor knows that beneath requests for tangible assistance there are often problems of fear and anxiety and guilt, nevertheless there is a place for the Church to take seriously, on their own level, the problems of social assistance which people bring to its attention. Sometimes this will require dividing responsibility with a social agency, so that the technical aspects of the need receive the most skilled attention while the spiritual orientation is also dealt with, and the whole relationship is a tripartite one where as far as possible there is mutual confidence all around. Sometimes this will require guidance from community resources, while the pastor himself continues to carry the primary responsibility of helping people work things through. Sometimes the whole situation must be referred to resources able to handle it, while the pastor maintains a friendly interest without being directly involved, lest the treatment be confused.

Worry About Children

Very often parents will turn to their minister when they are concerned about the behavior of their children. This is probably not so much because they expect him to have any special competence in the area of child problems, as that they believe him to be a friendly, sympathetic person who is reasonably well informed about these things. Sometimes the minister is brought into the picture in the belief that his intervention with school authorities, or even the police, will soften the punishment to which a child may be liable, or will get him off scot free.

Every kind of problem comes to the pastor's attention, but these can be grouped under the headings of relationship with parents, relationship with other children, and adjustment at school—both academic and disciplinary. If a family has a church relationship which means anything at all to them, the pastor will certainly be called in if a child is arrested.

In every instance involving the problems of children, the pastor should be acquainted with the resources in the community and therefore able to arrange for the most competent technical assistance—child guidance clinics, psychometric testing, remedial reading, special schools, camps, recreational facilities, and the like. Very often parents are frightened because they do not know that there are resources available to help them with specific problems, and are often reassured when they discover that such assistance is readily at hand. Again, the pastor may well be expected to make books available to help the parents gain insight both into themselves and into the reasons for the behavior of their children—such as those by Gesell and Spock, to name only two.

In this pastoral relationship there is a deeper issue in the ministry to parents who are anxious about the problems of their children: it is the Church's ministry to guilt. When a child fails in any area, it is only natural that the parents will seek to place the blame somewhere. If they cannot successfully attribute it to the child's peculiar temperament or an obtuse, insensitive teacher, or bad influences from other children or some other external source, they find themselves confronted with their own failure as parents. Even when they apparently succeed in projecting the blame for their child's problems on someone else or on unfortunate circumstances beyond control, still the haunting doubt remains that they have let their children down.

People feel guilty not only because they may be partly to blame for their children's difficulties; there is another side with which the pastor must be concerned. When children get into difficulty, causing worry and extra work for their parents, the parents often resent it and then feel guilty for harboring angry feelings toward their own children. The ministry of pastoral care in its specifically Christian aspect is addressed directly to this problem of guilt. It is recreant to its own purpose if it consists in trying to let people down easily. There is always an element of reality in the guilt, and there can be little redemption until this is faced for what it is. We do fail our children not once but often, and we don't stop doing it.

The Church speaks in terms of forgiveness, and this becomes concrete in a peculiarly realistic way where parents and children are involved. There is no better illustration of the Christian doctrine of grace than the fact that, even though we as parents fail our children, God does not discharge us as incompetent; he trusts us to learn from our experience and to grow in the quality of life which marks our relationships with them. Here is the way the Church deals creatively with the feelings of personal inadequacy which fathers and mothers so often have in their role as parents.

The Christian fellowship in its function as family of families undergirds the hopes of frail human agents who, as individuals, often find themselves over their depth in trying to be good parents. The Christian faith does not guarantee success in the sense that problems are eliminated or never arise again, but it does promise the grace to live creatively with the ever-changing pattern of relationships which is the way parents have to live with their children as the former grow older and the latter pass through the stages from infancy to adulthood.

Adoption and Placement

The minister will often be the first person consulted when a couple wishes to adopt a child or when a family feels the need for placing a member in an institution. If he is not the first person approached for help, if that family has any church connection at all, he will be involved in their situation before long.

While there are obviously many differences between seeking children for adoption and placing members of one's family in institutions, there is a basic similarity which is of importance in this study. In both types of situations people are tempted to think of other people as things, even though they don't intend to, even though they intend to become loving or to remain loving.

Because the baby to be adopted does not as yet have any personal existence within the family which seeks to find him—indeed he is "baby" as type rather than an individual until there is actually an adoption case in process —people tend at one and the same time to idealize this hypothetical child and to want a possession. The pastor's role, therefore, is more than assistance to a family in making contact with the most appropriate adoption agencies —warning them against those informal short-cuts through the normal procedures which, while they may produce a baby sooner, may also result in heartbreaks, and providing references for them to the agencies concerned. He has the major task of helping them to see this new relationship in the light of God's love. Adoption on the level of civil law is analogous to Holy Baptism in the life of the

Church—love creates a relationship because it cares, and personality lives and grows and finds its fulfillment within it.

The pastoral ministry to those contemplating adoption will necessarily have to help people understand the dangers involved, particularly those spiritual dangers of guilt in the parents when the child appears to reject the love they offer, and of resentment in the parents when the child's presence becomes a complication in planning rather than a source of joy. Parents feel guilt because of, and resentment toward, the behavior of their own children, yet adoptive parents are sometimes radically upset by finding they have the same feelings. Again, while the technical aspects of working through these feelings and relationships may require specially trained assistance, the pastor's role is once more that of making God's acceptance and forgiveness effective in the situation.

Problems of placement—whether of elderly relatives or even, more sadly, of limited children—begin with unhappiness and guilt. They are unlike the adoption situations, yet they have the same problem of tempting those responsible for placing others to think of them as things instead of persons. Indeed, people find that they have to make themselves turn these unfortunates into things in order to justify the placements, because they tell themselves that in an ideal world this should not have to happen. The pastor, again, has the responsibility not only of helping the family to make contact with the most appropriate nursing home or special school or whatever institution is called for, he must help them interpret what they are doing; and it is here that his specifically pastoral ministry is felt.

This ministry of pastoral care involves helping the people concerned to realize that there are limits to what can be done at this stage in the world's development—and of course there will still be limits even when social resources have advanced beyond what we now know. God does not expect his children to do the impossible. He expects them, on the other hand, to use those resources which have been developed for the care of the aging and the defective as his gifts. Men and women may not yet have developed these skills very far, and what is available may not be ideal, but it can be used by those who care as one of God's resources for loving his children. Furthermore, contact does not end when the person who needs placement has been received in the institution where he belongs. Love does not require actual physical encounters all the time, but through prayer and visits and such other connections as the situation permits, people who love may cross the physical barriers between persons. The pastor may also help those who have to make placements to live through the guilt they have felt for their own failures to meet every possible need, and even more for the resentment they have felt when these persons were burdens to them. In other words, here again is the ministry of acceptance, forgiveness, and love within God's Holy People with the minister serving as focus.

Economic Problems

Questions of economic need are dealt with last in this study, not because they are least important, but because in a way they can be used to tie the strings together in practical form. The ministry of pastoral care has to deal with the economic needs of people just because men and women are by virtue of creation economic creatures, with wants and needs which require the resources of society to satisfy. The fact that sometimes people are unable to sell their talents and services to pay for the other goods and services they need does not deny that they, like all other people—indeed like the pastor himself—are involved inextricably in an economic society.

When we recognize that economic need is basic, then the question is primarily one of how it shall be met. There are many reasons why individuals and families become unable to support themselves; and the study of these is largely the province of the social caseworker, although it may sometimes require the services of the psychiatrist and medical doctor. Regardless of the cause of the problem, the pastor is often the first person approached, for a variety of reasons; and people have the right to expect that he will hear what they have to say about their need. While they may not appreciate the framework in which he listens, still this encounter is first of all an evidence of God's concern for his children mediated through the minister.

It is one thing, however, for a clergyman to recognize the sacred significance of economic relationships and quite another thing for him to become the administrative agent through whom relief is granted. As a matter of fact, financial aid should be given by a church only in the direst emergency and on a temporary basis pending the working out of a more adequate social plan. This writer does not admire the Mormons for having kept all their members off the relief rolls during the depression. Men and women cannot be dependents of, and equal participants in, the same fellowship at one and the same time. The Church may meet economic distress quite acceptably on a secular level at the price of being unable any longer to serve as that fellowship in which a man dares to feel a sense of belonging on the sole basis of his own personhood.

The ministry to financial need usually involves relating the persons concerned to the private or public agency best equipped to deal with their problems. Under the law the community, through the Public Welfare Department, assumes basic responsibility for the care of the aged, the blind, the handicapped, and dependent children. There is also a gray area of economic need with a title "general relief" for which the public agency is usually responsible and for which it usually has inadequate funds. In helping people to work out questions of financial assistance, the resources of the Public Welfare Department are designed for this purpose and should be understood as natural community resources. No more stigma should be attached to receiving public assistance as provided under the law than to calling the fire department when there is a fire. The professional social worker is trained to help those with whom she works to accept assistance where it is really needed, because along with this will go long-range planning for the reorganization of individual and family financing.

Reference to both private and public agencies involves a real pastoral ministry as well as a transfer of immediate responsibility. In some situations, there will have been a refusal to accept reality by those who prefer to try to "sponge" from the churches, yet only sentimentality would insist that the clergyman should continue to give handouts rather than take steps leading to an end of the problem. In other situations there will be an anxiety as to what the agencies require and a fear of having to face embarrassing inquiries into private affairs; yet, again, these resources exist because the community needs them, and the minister can share the experience with the anxious person rather than simply pass him over to some stranger. In still other situations there will be a kind of false pride which makes people say they do not want charity, although they are perfectly willing to accept it from the church instead of a community agency, and here the pastoral ministry involves a study of reality in friendship and love.

137

There is a place within Christian society for borrowing from one another, provided that the granting of a loan is understood both by the lender and the borrower to involve some serious commitment to repayment. Loans as a euphemism for handouts cannot be regarded as other than destructive notes in the pastoral ministry to those in economic need. It does not help people to live in God's world as his children, particularly to find their place in the congregation of God's Holy People, to be led to cheat the Church as an institution, even with the connivance of a well meaning clergyman. If a grant-in-aid is called for, and cannot be secured from community resources, let it be called a grant-in-aid and not a loan, even though hopes may be expressed on the part of both pastor and receiver that it will be repaid. The pastoral ministry to those in economic need may involve at least a little basic honesty in the way people understand each other.

In the last analysis, the pastoral ministry to those asking financial aid illustrates everything this book has been trying to say. The technical aspects of the problem need to be taken seriously because they are the needs of real people; but at the same time those skills and resources which the community has developed can be used here as proper gifts of God. The pastor's primary task is to maintain that kind of relationship with people which enables them to accept as real the fact that God accepts them, forgives them, and loves them, and has a place for them—regardless of their problems—within the family of his children, the Holy Catholic Church.

A LIMITED BIBLIOGRAPHY

Erich Fromm, *The Art of Loving*. New York: Harper & Bros., 1956

Reuel L. Howe, *Man's Need and God's Action*. Greenwich: Seabury Press, 1953

Reuel L. Howe, *The Creative Years*. Greenwich: Seabury Press, 1959

Albert C. Outler, *Psychotherapy and the Christian Message*. New York: Harper & Bros., 1954

David E. Roberts, *Psychotherapy and the Christian View of Man*. New York: Scribner's Sons, 1950

Charles R. Stinnette, *Anxiety and Faith*. Greenwich: Seabury Press, 1955

Charles R. Stinnette, *Faith, Freedom and Selfhood*. Greenwich: Seabury Press, 1959

Gibson Winter, *Love and Conflict*. New York: Doubleday & Co., 1958